SARAH PALIN'S

Secret Diary

WARNING: This book is a parody. It has not been created, approved, licensed,
or sponsored by any former vice presidential candidate, any former governor
who resigned from office, any former mayor of any small town, any former
beauty pageant winner or runner-up, or the great state of Alaska.
Please be advised that this parody contains strong doses of irony and satire.
Consult a doctor to determine whether laughter is the best medicine for you.

Published by Lunatic Press, Los Angeles
www.lunaticpress.com

Cover photograph © 2006 by Jeff Medkeff.
Used by permission of Karen Medkeff and the Estate of Jeff Medkeff.

Book design by Joey Green
PRINTED IN THE UNITED STATES OF AMERICA

For Debbie

Thanks to John Firestone, Michael Gerber, Adam-Troy Castro,
Steve North, Jason Brightman, and Neil Sokoler.
All my love to Debbie, Ashley, and Julia.

Library of Congress Control Number 2009910098

ISBN: 0-9772590-4-8
ISBN-13: 978-0-9772590-4-8

10 9 8 7 6 5 4 3 2 1

SARAH PALIN'S

Secret Diary

Forged by
Joey Green

Lunatic Press
Los Angeles

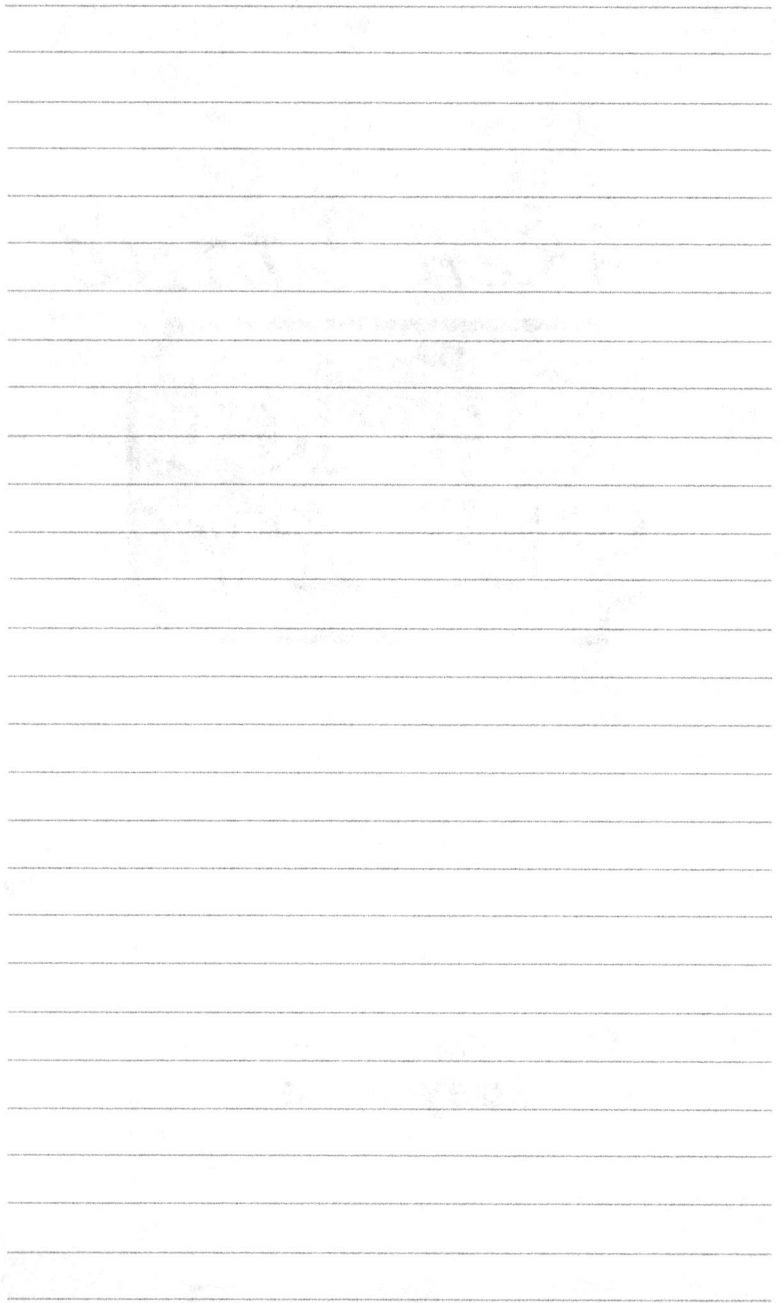

Dear Diary,

Goodness gracious, what a wild day!!!
Wow!!! I feel like I just finished racin' across
Alaska in the Iditarod!

Here I was totally psyched to give a keynote
speech at the Republican Governors Conference
there in Dallas, Texas, which would really help
put me on the map, and there was no way a
little thing like bein' 44-years old and eight-
months pregnant with a baby diagnosed with
Down Syndrome was gonna stop me from flyin'
from Alaska to Texas and back again. After
all, the baby wasn't due for another month,
I've already popped out four kids, and I'm the
world's best hockey mom. You betcha! I'm one
tough cookie. I'm a barracuda!

Besides, I was travelin' with my First Dude,
Todd, a four-time champion of the Iron Dog,
the world's toughest 2,000-mile snowmobile
race. What could possibly go wrong? Together,
we're unstoppable. Todd is a man's man. In
fact, he must have chugged four or five beers
on the plane. He's such a stud!!!

So when we got off the plane there in
Dallas, I never figured there was a snowball's
chance in hell that at 4 o'clock in the morning

I'd wake up in our hotel room to find myself sleepin' in a puddle of water. I figured Todd, that joker, was pullin' one of his practical jokes, but when I heard him snorin' like a moose, I realized that my water had actually broken. Not a gusher, just a slight leak. Holy cow! The last thing I wanted was for the baby to be born in Texas! If Alaska ever secedes from the United States, like Todd hopes, all of our kids have to be 100% Alaskan. Otherwise, this innocent little baby will be deported back to Texas! I was shakin' in my boots at the thought of this, even though I wasn't wearin' any boots because I was in bed.

The whole Alaska secession thing was freakin' me out, so I elbowed Todd. "Honey, we have a situation!" I said. Todd wasn't very happy that I woke him up. He was dreamin' that he was racin' his snowmobile in the 2,000-mile Iron Dog Race and he was comin' up on the finish line, runnin' neck and neck, and now he'd never know if he'd won the race or not — and he had a wicked hangover to boot (even though he wasn't wearin' boots either).

All of a sudden, I felt contractions — a month early, without any warnings! Whoa Nelly, I thought, I can't let this baby be born in

Texas! But there was no way I was gonna leave without givin' my speech! What do we do?

"Call your doctor," said Todd. "We can't have a salmon picker born in Texas!"

I picked up the telephone and called my doctor back in Alaska.

"What were you doin' flyin' in the first place?" Cathy asked. "Earth to Sarah! You're eight-months pregnant! You're not supposed to fly on an airplane."

"Well, how was I supposed to know that?"

"It says so in all the books. You've had four children. Haven't you read the books?"

"Of course, I've read the books," I said. I didn't wanna seem like an idiot, even though I haven't read any of those books. To tell you the truth, I find them obscene. The pictures are really lewd, and if it was up to me, I'd ban them from the library. "I just don't remember readin' anything about airplanes," I said. There certainly weren't any pictures of airplanes in those books. The closest thing to an airplane was a drawin' of a dingdong, but it didn't have any wings, propellers, or landin' gear.

"You should have asked me," Cathy said.

"I didn't wanna bother you with such trivial questions like whether it was safe to fly."

I told her all about that there Republican Governors Conference and how cool it was that I was scheduled to give the keynote speech at the luncheon.

"How'd you even get on the plane?" she asked. "Most airlines forbid women in their last month of pregnancy to fly."

"Not Alaska Airlines. They didn't ask. I didn't tell. Gosh, I'm hardly showin'—not like those gals who look like they swallowed a baby whale or somethin'. So I wore a big coat and some colorful scarves to cover it up."

"Sarah, you could have gone into labor with a special needs child during the flight—without a doctor or nurse."

"I feel fine," I insisted. "I leaked some water, that's all, and I'm feelin' some contractions."

"Contractions?!? Sarah, call an ambulance. You need to get to a hospital there in Dallas to have the fluid tested and see how far along labor is."

"The contractions really aren't that bad. There's only like one or two an hour." I've given birth to four kids. I know what labor feels like, and I knew I wasn't in labor. "I'm gonna stay for the day," I said. "I have a thirty-minute speech to give that could really launch me to the big time. Wild horses couldn't stop me from givin' that speech."

"All right then, go ahead and give the speech," said Cathy. "But until then, put up your feet and rest."

I did more than put my feet up. I shoved a roll of toilet paper up there to stop the baby from comin' out.

At noon, I gave the speech, which was really awesome, and then I ran from the podium. Todd and I raced to the airport, and we jumped on an Alaska Airlines plane for the four-hour flight to Seattle. There's no way the airline woulda let me fly if they had known I was havin' contractions, so I figured "what they don't know won't hurt them."

When we landed in Seattle, we coulda gone to a hospital, but bein' born there in Washington State is way worse than bein' born in Texas. Todd said if our baby was born in Seattle, we'd have to name him Starbucks. Besides, it was only a two-hour layover in Seattle and just another four-hour flight to Alaska. So, I went in the bathroom and shoved another roll of toilet paper up there. This baby was gonna be born an Alaskan citizen, because there's no way Todd and I are gonna raise a son named Starbucks. And they were showin' the movie

SNOW DOGS, starrin' Cuba Gooding, Jr., on the plane, and I've always wanted to see that movie, which I have to say was just darlin'! When the movie ended, I went to the bathroom in the back of the plane and shoved another roll of toilet paper up there.

We finally landed here in Anchorage at around 10:30 at night, and we coulda driven straight to the nearest hospital, but I really can't stand city folk, so I hopped on the back of Todd's Arctic Cat snowmobile and we raced the 45 miles to the Mat-Su Regional Medical Center in Palmer, just a ways down the road from our house.

At 6:30 this morning, I gave birth to three rolls of toilet paper and a beautiful baby boy weighin' 6 pounds, 2 ounces. Of all my deliveries, I have to say this was by far the easiest of them all. It was much smoother than givin' birth to Track in an igloo with a toothless Eskimo midwife, poppin' out Bristol on the back of a dog-sled racin' across the tundra, goin' into labor with Willow while trekkin' across Hubbard Glacier, or deliverin' Piper on an ice float in the Arctic Ocean.

We are truly blessed that Trig was born in the great state of Alaska!

- Eskimo Kingdom
- Arctic Free Zone
- Freezeland
- The Tundra Territory
- The Permafrost Empire
- Land of Oil
- The Frostbite Federation
- New Siberia
- The Republic of Alaska
- West Canada
- Sarahland
- Palinstan ✓✓✓

APRIL 19, 2008

Dear Diary,

We named the baby Trig Paxson Van Palin after the fact that neither Todd nor I ever took trigonometry in school, so this way, folks will think we love trigonometry. Paxson is for the town of Paxson, Alaska, where Todd loves to go snowmobilin' and where I love to shoot moose. And Van because we both love Van Halen, and we thought it would be funny to name our kid Van Palin, but at the last minute we chickened out and added on Trig and Paxson, so no one would really notice the Van Palin, except us. So it's our little inside joke. When I'm breastfeedin', Todd keeps pokin' his head into the room singin' the Van Halen song "And the Cradle Will Rock"!

He's such a he-man. We just thank our lucky stars we didn't have to name the baby Lone Star or Starbucks.

I'm so proud that all our kids have such cool names. We named Track after the fact that he was born durin' track season and because my Dad coached track. If Track had been born durin' basketball season, I woulda named him Hoop. If he'd been born durin' baseball season, he woulda been named Batt. During football season: Tackle. And during hockey season: Puck.

Most folks think we named our daughter Bristol after Bristol Bay in Alaska, where Todd grew up and fishes for salmon, and because I worked at the Bristol Inn. But the truth is—Bristol is named after Bristol, Connecticut, the city of my dreams. When I was workin' as a sportscaster for KTUU-TV there in Anchorage, I dreamed of workin' for ESPN—until I discovered that ESPN is based far, far away in Bristol, Connecticut. Oh well. No biggie. So, instead of movin' to Bristol, I did the next best thing. I named my first baby girl after the city. She's also named after Bristol-Myers, the company that makes Pepto-Bismol. I didn't realize until a few years later that Bristol-

Myers doesn't make Pepto-Bismol. Procter & Gamble does. So I guess Bristol should really be named Procter.

Our daughter Willow is named after the Alaska state bird—the willow ptarmigan. Todd wanted to name her Ptarmigan, but to me, that sounds too much like some kind of dinosaur cheese. Plus, that's a really hard name for a kid to spell. So I said let's name her after the state tree, the Sitka Spruce. "Hey, the willow is also a tree," said Todd. So we met halfway and named the baby Willow.

We named our daughter Piper Indy after the fact that Todd flies a 1958 Piper Cub plane that we just love, and her middle name comes from the Polaris Indy, the snowmobile Todd drove in the first of his four victories in the Iron Dog snowmobile race. I just thank the Lord that Todd didn't fly a Cessna and ride a Bombardier.

APRIL 20, 2008

Dear Diary,

Boy, oh boy! Last night, the Russians were makin' so much noise. They must have been throwin' one of their communist parties. They were hollerin' and screamin' and singin' and throwin' vodka bottles. What a racket! I could

• 13 •

hear their shenanigans all the way up there in our bedroom on the other side of the house.

I had just finished feedin' Trig and gettin' him to sleep, and I was about to pick up the phone to call Vladimir Putin and ask him if he could please pipe down over there and give us Alaskans a little peace and quiet, but I figured I'd better check it out before makin' any accusations that might upset the balance of power. So I put on a bathrobe and slippers and went downstairs to take a closer look from the kitchen window — where I have a pretty good view of Russia — to see what in God's name those darn Ruskies were up to.

Well, I looked out the window, and there in the backyard was Bristol and a bunch of her high school friends shootin' their rifles at a stack of beer kegs stacked up on the far side of the lawn. Talk about Alaska Wildlife! Her boyfriend Levi Johnston was out there, too, wearin' his hockey uniform, holdin' up his hockey stick in one hand, and spinnin' in circles. He'd stop, wobble around, and then fall to the ground, yellin' "I'm a f***in' redneck! A f***in' redneck! Don't f*** with a f***in' redneck!" That boy is dumb as a doorknob, but I gotta admit, he's one hunk of a hottie.

"Bistol, honey, what the heck is goin' on out there?" I asked.

"Mom, it's those darn Russians again," she said. "We're just firin' off warnin' shots to keep them away."

That's my girl!

Dear Diary,

Maternity leave is for sissies. It's great to be back at work! I can't believe the Alaska State Court banned my offer to pay $150 to every hunter who hacks off the left foreleg of a wolf shot from a plane. The wolves have been killin' the moose and caribou, gosh darn it! We hunters are supposed to be the ones killin' the moose and caribou. Now we hunters have to kill the wolves, so we can kill the moose and caribou. It's God's will that we should be shootin' the wolves from planes. That's why God created planes and AK-47s. We gotta kill, baby, kill!

Those darn scientists say that the number of wolves have no impact on the number of moose and caribou, but how is anyone on God's good earth supposed to believe scientists with all their hogwash about evolution? I mean, honestly. That's why last year I spent $400,000 in taxpayer money to educate the public about the advantages of shootin' wolves and bears from the air. I should get the State of Alaska to pay $150 to every hunter who kills a scientist!

Dear Diary,

Call me crazy, but I just don't like anyone messin' with my little sister. I love Molly to pieces, I really do. But jeepers-creepers, what was she thinkin' when she married that train wreck Mike Wooten? I mean, Good Golly, Miss Molly! You were his fourth wife! The guy had already struck out three times! Is it really any surprise that he cheated on ya with another woman? Wooten is a genuine creep, let me tell ya. The psycho tasered my ten-year-old nephew Payton—right there in front of Bristol! Wooten showed the kid his Taser, and when the boy pleaded to be tasered, Wooten taped

PRIZES for SHOOTIN' WOLVES FROM AIRPLANES

⭐ 20 OR MORE — Trip to Republican National Convention

⭐ 15 WOLVES — A Wasilla High School Diploma

⭐ 12 WOLVES — A ride on the back of Todd's snowmobile

⭐ 10 WOLVES — Tickets to the Alaska Gun Show

⭐ 8 WOLVES — The key to the City of Wasilla

⭐ 5 WOLVES — A free rape test kit for the rape victim of your choice

⭐ 1 WOLF — A subscription to the ANCHORAGE DAILY NEWS

the probes to him and gave him a blast of the Taser for a second. The jolt knocked the kid backward, which scared the bejeebers out of Bristol. What a freakazoid! He's trailer trash. But then, so is Molly, bless her heart.

Todd and I have tried everything possible to get Wooten fired—with no luck whatsoever. So tonight, Todd telephoned the Mug-Shot Saloon and, when he found out that Wooten was there, he hopped on his Arctic Cat snowmobile and rode over to Mike Wooten's house to toilet paper all the trees and bushes there in his yard. That Todd! He's such a wild man! I love him to pieces. I wanted to go with him, but I'm sittin' here breastfeedin' Trig, and Todd didn't want me breastfeedin' Trig on the back of the snowmobile, coz then there wouldn't be enough room for the big box of Charmin that he had strapped onto the back of the seat. Todd was like, "Wooten will never suspect it was us because we just had a baby!"

Wooten is a tickin' time bomb, a loose cannon, a frickin' whack job. He shouldn't be an Alaska State Trooper, that's for sure. He drank beer while drivin' his Trooper car. He shot a moose without a hunting license. And he chews gum with his mouth open.

I'll never forget that day in February 2005 when Molly accused Wooten of cheatin' on her, and she put me on speakerphone so I could hear everything. Molly told Wooten that our Daddy was gonna hire an attorney to help her with the divorce. Wooten hollered, "I will kill him. He'll eat a f***in' lead bullet, I'll shoot him." I couldn't believe what I was hearin' and neither could Track, who was listenin' with me.

I was so scared for Molly that I hopped in the car, drove to her house, stood there in the driveway, and watched through a window. I could see Wooten wearin' his Trooper gun on his hip and wavin' his arms like a maniac.

I thought he was gonna totally lose it, but I had a meetin' to get to, and frankly, my political career is much more important than Molly's domestic squabbles, so I drove off.

Daddy filed a police report, and Todd and I have done everything possible to get that dimwit fired. I sent a three-page e-mail to the head of the state police, tellin' her that Wooten was a one-man terrorist cell. I even sent Todd over to try to talk some sense into the doofus. But later that day, the phone rings and it's Molly, shakin' like a leaf. Wooten told her that she'd better "put a leash on your sister" or else he'll "bring Sarah Palin down." What a nincompoop! No one can bring this hockey mom down.

A judge reviewed all the complaints filed by my family, but at the trial he said he couldn't understand why we were tryin' to get Wooten fired, since deprivin' the numbskull of a job could prevent him from payin' family support to Molly. C'mon, judge! Wooten can always get a job moppin' the restrooms at the Mug-Shot Saloon. A few months later, the head of the state police said that Wooten's conduct as a State Trooper was kooky. Duh!!! She suspended him from his job for five days. Five measly days?!? Ya gotta be kiddin' me!

Wooten deserves to have toilet paper all over his trees and bushes. So does the head of the state police, come to think of it. I'm gonna call Todd on his cell phone and tell him to save some toilet paper! Nobody messes with Sarah Barracuda! Nobody!

APRIL 26, 2008

Dear Diary,

I'm really worried about Bristol and Levi! I walked into Bristol's room tonight to find the room lit with at least 100 candles around Bristol's bed—on the floor, on the furniture, on the window sills—and Bristol and Levi were lyin' on the bed, completely naked, readin' a big hardcover book together. Levi's face turned white, Bristol quickly shut the book, and the two of them pulled up the covers on the bed to hide their nakedness and the book, but before they did, I saw the title of the book, which was something weird like THE KAMA SUTRA. It was my worst nightmare come true. I didn't mince words.

"Are you two practicin' some sort of Satanism?" I demanded.

"Uh, no, Mom, we're not practicin' Satanism," said Bristol. "I don't even know what Satanism is."

"Look, I know Satanism when I see it," I said, firmly. "All these candles, the book of witchcraft you're hidin' under the covers, the fact that you're both naked. You two are in very dangerous territory."

"You're right, Mrs. Palin," said Levi. "I checked out a book from the library and we were just tryin' out a few things."

I knew I shoulda banned a whole bunch of books from that gosh-darn library when I had the chance as Mayor.

So, I closed the door and sat down on the edge of the bed, and the three of us had a long talk about the evils of Satanism. The kids took an oath to never practice Satanism again, and Levi promised to return the book to the library right away. Phew! What a scare!

APRIL 29, 2008

Dear Diary,

I love my Public Safety Commissioner, Walt Monegan, I really do. But doggone it! I had no idea that he'd be such a tough nut to crack. When I became Governor, I appointed Monegan to be my Public Safety Commissioner because he had been Anchorage Police Chief for five years. I figured that Monegan was the kind of grandfatherly, straight-arrow guy with a Magnum P.I. mustache who wouldn't want some screwball like Mike Wooten as a State Trooper. It's been almost a year and a half now, and Monegan still hasn't done diddlysquat about Wooten. I just don't understand it.

Durin' my first month in office, Todd invited Monegan to the Governor's office and gave him a thick file on Wooten that he put together with a private investigator who we hired to follow Wooten around. But Monegan told him there was nothin' he could do. I called Monegan a few days later on his cell phone, but he told me the same thing. I brought it up again in February 2007 there in the state capitol building and Monegan warned me to stay at arm's length. He was lookin' at me like I was some wild-eyed bitch on wheels, I could tell. I backed off, but every now and then I'd bring up the topic in an e-mail, sayin' things like, "That Wooten is a real bonehead," or "That State Trooper I used to be related to sure makes State Troopers look like total goofballs," or "You're a real trooper—unlike that doofus who used to be married to my sister."

It's time to crank up the volume to get Monegan to do the right thing!

POSSIBLE GIFTS FOR MONEGAN

TO ENTICE HIM TO FIRE WOOTEN

- Moose Burgers (set up grill in his office)
- Miss Wasilla trophy
- Bear skin rug from my office
- Wolf pelts
- Tour of Todd's BP Refinery on North Slope
- Be Todd's teammate in next Iron Dog snowmobile race
- A date with my sister Molly

I brought Trig into work with me because I'm breastfeedin' the little ball of joy, just like I did with Piper, so I decided to bring Trig over for Monegan to see my cute little bundle of sweetness.

"Do ya like him?" I asked.

"He's adorable," said Monegan. "Can I keep him?"

"Absolutely," I said. "All ya gotta do is fire a certain State Trooper who shall remain unnamed, and Trig is all yours."

Monegan chuckled and handed Trig back to me.

"Or maybe ya want something more," I said, unbuttonin' my blouse.

"What are you doing?" asked Monegan.

"Feedin' time," I said, takin' out one of my boobies to feed Trig. "Just pick up the phone, Walt, and all this can be yours."

Monegan's jaw dropped to the floor and his face turned white. It was hysterical. I told Todd all about it, figurin' we'd share a good laugh, but he stormed out the backdoor and shot a coyote that happened to be runnin' through our yard. Oh well.

MAY 4, 2008

Dear Diary,

So I drove home from work, pulled into the driveway, took Trig out of his baby seat and carried the little cutie patootie into the house. Suddenly, I hear clankin' and bangin' comin' from the basement. I put Trig in his baby swing and told Piper and Willow to watch him, and I took off my heels and went downstairs into the basement to see what all the racket was about.

Bristol was standin' at a table, stirrin' whatever was boilin' there in a huge pot on an electric burner. On the table sat all sorts of pots, pans, and buckets, packets of malt and hops, thermometers, siphons, and other stuff.

"What in the world are you two doin'?" I asked, still worried about Satanism.

"Stirrin' the wort so it doesn't boil over," said Bristol.

"I'm rehydratin' the yeast," said Levi.

"Isn't this cool?" asked Bristol. "We're makin' beer." She pointed to the clean, empty glass beer bottles sittin' in a wooden case on the floor.

"Beer?" I asked. "Why are ya makin' beer?"

"For science class," said Bristol. "It's our science project."

"Yeah," said Levi. "It's our science project."

"It's all about fermentation," said Bristol.

"Yeah," said Levi. "Fermentation."

I'm so proud of those two kids. They worked all night long on that science project. There were all sorts of bangs and screams and moans and squeals of delight comin' from the basement into the wee hours of the night. They really worked hard.

MAY 7, 2008

Dear Diary,

I let Todd use the phone in my office all day. He opened the Yellow Pages and called every pizza parlor, caterer, phone company, plumber, gas company, exterminator, and construction company in Wasilla. He told them that he was

Mike Wooten and asked them to all arrive at his house at 11 a.m. tomorrow morning`! I love Todd to pieces. He's incredible!

Dear Diary,

Todd and I drove by Wooten's house at 11:15 a.m. to find the street filled with vans and trucks from Piccolinos Restaurant, Pizza Time, Enstar Natural Gas Company, Matanuska Telephone Association, and almost every business in Wasilla.

Tons of angry folks were standin' there in front of Wooten's house. Wooten was hollerin' and screamin', throwin' his arms in the air, and his face was all red. It was funnier than the time Todd drove his pick-up truck across the frozen lake and the ice cracked and the truck fell into the lake.

Dear Diary,

I made up my own lyrics and choreographed my own dance steps to the ABBA Song "Super Trouper," taught it all to my Chief of Staff Mike Tibbles and my Attorney General Talis Colberg, and then the three of us dressed up

in Alaska State Trooper uniforms, burst into
Monegan's office, hit play on our portable
Karaoke machine, and began singin' . . . .

Stupid Trooper, no need to remind me
Your days here are through!
Time to say adieu!
'Cause somehow I'll get rid of you!

I'm so sick and tired of your abuse!
Like how you cheated on my little sister!
You broke the state law and shot a moose!
Just who do you think you are, mister?
(Just who do you think you are, mister?)
When you're on duty, there's no drinkin' beer
    and drivin'!
(No sir, we ain't jivin'!)
Ain't no way you'll bring me down!
(And ain't no way you're gonna shoot)
You ain't gonna shoot my father
Before you're run out of town!

Tonight the
Stupid Trooper's Taser's gonna blind me
Like the midnight sun!
(Stup-p-pid Troop-p-per)
Turn in your badge and gun!

(Stup-p-pid Troop-p-per)
We wanna see your work here done!
Tonight the
Stupid Trooper's squad car's gonna find me
But I just don't care!
(Stup-p-pid Troop-p-per)
You don't have a prayer!
(Stup-p-pid Troop-p-per)
We'll feed you to a polar bear!

MAY 13, 2008

Dear Diary,

When I got home from the office tonight, Todd was sittin' there in the Laz-E-Boy rocker, finishin' off the last bottle from a six-pack of Alaska Amber. When he saw me come in, he began singin', "And the Cradle Will Rock"! I had no idea why he was in such a great mood, until he told me the awesome news.

While I was at work, Todd drove over to Mike Wooten's house, placed a paper bag filled with dog poop on his front porch, lit the bag on fire, rang the doorbell, and ran away. From the bushes, he watched Wooten open the front door and stomp on the flamin' bag with his freshly polished Trooper boots.

Todd is the coolest!

MAY 14, 2008

Dear Diary,

Of all the nerve! Today, the U.S. Department of the Interior listed the Polar Bear as a threatened species. That is _soooo_ ridiculous! This totally gets in the way of drillin' for oil. Those darn polar bears live on Alaska's northern and northwestern coasts—on the exact spots where we need to drill, baby, drill!

Those hoity-toity left-wing liberal egghead scientists—with their evolution and global warming and phony scientific malarkey—are always doctorin' their smarty-pants charts and maps and graphs to foist their left-wing liberal agenda on the unsuspectin' public! So what if last year the arctic sea ice shrunk to the smallest area ever recorded by satellite? So what if the sea ice has shrunk 39%? So what if sea ice is crucial to polar bear survival? There's nothin' to worry about! We're just headed to the End of Days, like the Bible predicts. Anything we can do to speed that along will bring us closer to the Day of Judgment, and that's truly a blessin' for everyone, includin' the polar bears.

Besides, the number of polar bears has practically doubled over the last thirty years.

Just because their habitat is meltin' doesn't mean that the polar bears will all drown in the Arctic Ocean. Sheesh. We can always load all those polar bears (and scientists!) on a big ship and drop them off in Russia when nobody's looking. Problem solved!

Ya know who the real threatened species is? The oil companies, that's who.

HOW TO MAKE HUNTIN' MORE EXCITIN'

▶ CLUSTER BOMB POLAR BEARS
▶ SHOOT BAZOOKAS AT BALD EAGLES
▶ THROW BOWLIN' BALLS AT BABY SEALS
▶ FIRE CANNONBALLS AT CARIBOU
▶ SHOOT ROCKET-PROPELLED GRENADES AT MOOSE

MAY 15, 2008

Dear Diary,

I think Monegan has gone completely psycho. Today was Police Memorial Day, and just before the annual celebration, he dropped off a poster at my office for me to autograph and present at the ceremony. The poster was a color picture of an Alaska State Trooper salutin' in front of the police memorial there in

Anchorage. When I looked closer, I recognized the Trooper in the picture. It was that lowlife Wooten! I couldn't believe it!

I made my assistant call Monegan to get to the bottom of this, but Monegan said it was an innocent mistake. He didn't realize the Trooper in the photo was Wooten. Oh yeah, sure. And all my phone calls to his office are just me dialin' a wrong number. Puh-lease! So I cancelled my appearance and sent Lieutenant Governor Parnell there in my place. While Monegan was sittin' through Parnell's tedious speech (the guy is such a windbag, bless his heart!), Todd and I were out toilet papering Monegan's house!!!

MAY 17, 2008

Dear Diary,

This afternoon I walked into Bristol's room to ask her to baby-sit Trig so I could take a nap. OMG! She was wearin' a hot-pink leopard print bustier with lace trim, white stockings with black lace garters, black elbow-length gloves, and stiletto heels. She was seesawin' a pink feather boa between her legs.

Levi was lyin' on her bed, wearin' black leather hot pants and a matchin' vest, a black cowboy hat and a pair of cowboy boots.

I nearly fainted.

"What in the world is goin' on in here?" I asked.

"Uh, nothin', Mom," said Bristol. "We're just, uh, gettin' ready for a costume party."

"You really had me goin' there for a minute," I said. "But I know you two have taken a pledge of abstinence."

"Sure, Mom," said Bristol.

"Yeah," said Levi.

They're really good kids. I do hope they win a prize for best costume. They deserve it!

MAY 20, 2008

Dear Diary,

Todd opened up another can of whoop-ass on Mike Wooten tonight. Todd's background as a commercial salmon fisherman really came in handy. While Wooten was drinkin' at the Mug-Shot Saloon, Todd found Wooten's patrol car parked out front and tossed a dead salmon on the floor of the backseat. How cool is that?

MAY 22, 2008

Dear Diary,

My Attorney General Talis Colberg is so awesome. He wrote his dissertation for his Ph.D. on "M.D. Snodgrass: The Founder of the

MORE TRICKS TO PLAY ON WOOTEN
(All in Good Fun)

* TOSS A DEAD SKUNK IN HIS WINDOW.
* PUT A CASE OF BEER ON THE FRONT SEAT OF HIS PATROL CAR, SO UNABLE TO RESIST, HE'LL DRINK IT AND GET BUSTED FOR DRUNK DRIVIN'.
* USE HIS STATE-ISSUED CELL PHONE TO CALL SOME 900 NUMBERS.
* RELEASE THE PARKING BREAK AND ROLL HIS STATE TROOPER CAR IN FRONT OF A BROTHEL.
* BREAK INTO HIS HOUSE AND SHORT SHEET HIS BED.

Alaska State Fair." He's so smart! Today he and I came up with a really nifty plan to fight those boneheads there in the Department of the Interior. The State of Alaska is suin' the federal government to get polar bears off the threatened species list. Is that genius or what? The Department of the Interior isn't gonna stop this can-do hockey mom from drillin' for oil, that's for sure. All we gotta say is that their scientific evidence is all smoke and mirrors. It's insufficient voodoo. It's just a dumb theory like evolution or relativity or the Big Bang. Oh yeah, baby! And the cradle will rock! You betcha!

Dear Diary,

Poor Bristol was so sick this morning. She was pukin' her little guts out there in the bathroom. I hope she hasn't come down with a stomach virus or something. I asked her if I should call a doctor, but she said no, she'd be okay.

Then I remembered the beer that she and Levi were brewin' there in the basement for their science project. I went down there to check, but the beer was still there in the fermentor — all sealed — and the bottles were still empty, thank heavens. At least I know she has the brains to keep away from alcohol.

Bristol was feelin' better by lunchtime, and she went out to watch Levi play in a hockey game. Go Wasilla High School Warriors! When Bristol left the house, I went into her room to put away some laundry and I saw that she left her computer on. Levi's MySpace page was on the screen, so I sat down and scrolled through it. He really is adorable, except he uses the f-word a little too much, but he's just a typical teenager, I guess.

On his profile, he calls himself "a f***in' redneck" and says he enjoys "f***in' chillin'" and "Ya f**** with me I'll kick ass." He really is a little macho stud. He reminds me of Todd at that age. So cute!!!!

Dear Diary,

This morning, Monegan nearly freaked out! He walked into his office at 9 a.m. to find a human skeleton sittin' there in his chair and wearin' a State Trooper hat and badge. I had no idea that Todd borrowed a life-size model of a human skeleton from the Biology Department at Wasilla High School. He's such a joker! Monegan didn't find it very funny.

"C'mon, Walt," I said. "Where's your sense of humor? Wooten's made death threats against my family, for goodness sake. Fire the goofball already."

I mean, really, what more do we have to do? Todd and I have gotten every livin' soul in the gosh-darn Governor's office to telephone Monegan and pester him to get rid of the stupid Trooper. They've called his office, left messages on his voice mail, and put Post-it notes all over his car. We even had Piper and Willow call Monegan at home and ask if his refrigerator is runnin'.

But Monegan keeps sayin' that nothin' can be done and that harassin' Wooten could give the Stupid Trooper grounds to sue the State of Alaska. What if Wooten pulls over one of my kids and throws a bag of dope in the back seat just to frame a Palin? How do we convince Monegan that Wooten is a total nutjob?

Todd came up with a great idea this afternoon. He asked the computer guy in my office to help him hack into the computers at Blockbuster Video in Wasilla. They added a whole bunch of gay porn flicks to Wooten's records and then e-mailed it from the Blockbuster server to Monegan's e-mail address. Todd is _soooooo_ creative! I just love him to pieces! I really do!

MAY 30, 2008

Dear Diary,

Bristol was throwin' up again this morning. It really has me worried. I remember when I was competin' in the Miss Alaska Beauty Pageant that some of the other girls would lock themselves in the bathroom and make themselves throw up whatever they just ate because they didn't wanna risk not fittin' into their tight evening gowns or swimsuits. I'm sure that's why I only came in second place in the Miss Alaska Pageant. I mean, if anyone deserved to win, it was little ol' me. But how was I supposed to compete with a bunch of bulimics? I sure hope Bristol isn't makin' herself hurl to make herself thin for Levi.

NOTE TO SELF: Tell Bristol my story of the Miss Alaska Pageant.

JUNE 3, 2008

Dear Diary,

Todd is ingenious! He hired a bunch of theater majors from the University of Alaska, dressed them up in hockey uniforms, and had them march into Monegan's office. They told Monegan that they were the players on the hockey team that Mike Wooten coaches and that he had molested each one of them. Monegan almost fell for it, until he called up Wooten and discovered that the kids he coaches are all ten years old—not college age. What a bummer!

When Monegan figured out that Todd had planned this little charade, he had the police lock up all the actors there in the Anchorage Jail—and instructed them to call Todd to bail them out. Too bad Monegan forgot one thing.

Todd's married to the Governor, who can just call up the jail and give the kids a Governor's pardon. Tee hee hee!

Dear Diary,

When I told my staff to make sure that Todd gets copies of every e-mail sent from my office no matter how confidential, I didn't mean for him to get so much spam about penis enlargement! Sheesh! The idea is to make Todd feel big, not small!

I gotta have a talk with my staff! They have no idea how difficult it is bein' Governor and makin' Todd feel like the king of the castle. They don't understand how high maintenance he is. I gotta make him feel like he's in the loop on everything. He needs to feel like my knight in shinin' armor all the time. If I get e-mails criticizin' the way I do things, Todd needs to get copies, so he can come to my rescue. When I get e-mails about oil pipelines and refineries, I want copies sent to Todd so he feels important and needed. (And I really do need his help to understand all that complicated stuff! Yikes!) Todd's gotta be my First Dude, my stud-muffin, my Alaskan king crab—otherwise he feels like a clubbed baby seal, a beached whale, a lone wolf shot from a plane.

Thank the Lord that invitation arrived today asking him to be a judge for the 2008 Miss Alaska Pageant! That seemed to help him get over all those e-mails about penis enlargement. Just his gettin' the invitation worked like Viagra! I sure am glad I arranged that!!!

JUNE 12, 2008

Dear Diary,

Tonight, Bristol, her best friend Angie, Levi, Willow, and Piper were all sittin' on the couch watchin' HANNAH MONTANA, and suddenly Bristol invited Todd and me to come sit on the couch with them. When the show ended, Bristol picked up the remote and turned off the TV and told Willow and Piper to go upstairs.

Bristol looked sick to her stomach. "Are you okay, Bristol?" I asked. "You're all pale and you look like you're gonna hurl. Maybe we should getcha to a doctor."

"Mom, what's the worst thing that you can imagine?" asked Bristol.

Well, gosh, there are so many horrible things I can imagine. Mike Wooten becomin' Chief of Police. Evolution bein' taught in our schools by married gay couples. Women bein' allowed to have abortions just because they were raped by an uncle. Not bein' able to go huntin' for moose because the government has taken away our AK-47s. Not bein' able to drill, baby, drill, or kill, baby, kill! Wavin' that white flag of surrender in Iraq. Or gettin' a run in my stockings durin' the ribbon cuttin' ceremony for the Bridge to Nowhere. Finally, I said, "Barack Obama or Hillary Clinton bein' elected Mayor of Wasilla."

Bristol looked to me and then to Todd and then to Levi and then back to me and back to Todd and back to Levi.

Suddenly, her best friend Angie blurted out, "Bristol's pregnant."

I cracked up laughin'. "Good one," I said.

"How much of that beer down there in the basement did you three drink?" asked Todd.

"No, really. Bristol's pregnant," said Angie.

"Don't be ridiculous. Bristol's taken a pledge of abstinence. Didn't ya honey?"

Bristol shook her head yes, then no, then yes again.

"She's pregnant, Mrs. Palin," said Angie. "She's got a bun in the oven. She's on stork watch. The Pop-Tart is in the toaster. She's knocked up. She's totally pregnacious."

"Thanks, Angie," said Bristol. "I think my Mom gets the picture."

"There's gotta be some sort of mistake," I said. "You took an oath of abstinence."

"Well, it looks like Levi slipped one past the goalie," said Angie.

Levi thrust his arms in the air, and I thought he was about to do the wave. His eyes caught mine, and with his arms still in the air, he opened his mouth and faked a big yawn.

"Are ya absolutely sure?" I asked.

Bristol told us how she missed her period weeks ago, and that she took a pregnancy test like a gazillion times and it came up positive all gazillion times.

"Well, now you and the f***in' redneck are gonna have to grow up a lot faster than ya ever imagined," I said. "You two better work out a game plan."

"I decided I'm gonna have the baby," said Bristol, as if there was ever any question about that. Thank heavens she came to that decision on her own so I didn't have to make that decision for her. I'm as pro-life as any pro-life person can be, and if Bristol wasn't pro-life too, I woulda killed her. Bristol knows that I only believe in abortion in cases where the mother's life is in danger. Of course, if Bristol had said she wanted an abortion, her life woulda definitely been in danger.

Todd reached for the shotgun hangin' on the wall over the fireplace, took it down, and started polishin' it. "And what are your plans now, Levi?" he asked.

"Sure, I'd love to go huntin'," said Levi. "Let's kill some stuff."

"I mean your plans with Bristol," said Todd, aimin' the barrel of the shotgun at Levi's gorgeous face.

"Oh, that," said Levi. "Well, if it's okay with you and Governor Palin, I think maybe we should get married."

"Maybe?" asked Todd, cockin' the trigger.

"Definitely," said Levi.

"You really wanna marry my daughter, Levi?"

"Yeah, absolutely."

I was so excited. Todd's the First Dude. Now we're gonna have the First Slacker.

Todd lowered the shotgun. "Well, first there's a little something I need you to do for me," said Todd.

"Sure," said Levi. "Anything."

Todd is so resourceful! I can't wait to find out what he's got planned!!!

BABY NAMES FOR BRISTOL'S BABY
(Duh! That's Why They're Baby Names!)

BRATT	FRIDG	SPORE
SPARK	SPORK	THORN
PLUGG	TRICK	FUDD
TORCH	TREAT	SMOGG
PHART	SYRUP	DRIPP
SPLATT	DRECK	PLACK
BRILLO	GLITCH	SLACK
~~TROOPER~~	SLURPEE	SHRUGG
SPURT	SHARPIE	FLECK
SPIGOT	SLAPPY	MULCH
WIDGET	SPAGG (short	SKULL
SPROCKET	for Spaghetti)	MUCK
GORP	SPLEEN	SPUDD
FRIPP	ASPARAGUS	BORSCHT
FRAPP	(nickname "Gus")	FRATT
ALGEBRA (nickname	TURNIP	MANGO
"Algae"—so cute!)	SLINKY	IRVING
CALC (the perfect	SNAKE	CRISCO
follow-up to Trig)	ANGINA	CHEWBACCA
SNOWFLAKE	SLUSH	PYREX
BLIZZ (short for	SPOONS	FIZZ
Blizzard)	SLICK	THRUSH
ZORT	DUDD	GALEN (rhymes
SPRIGG	SLUGG	with Palin!)

Dear Diary,

Todd really outdid himself tonight! He drove the kids over to Mike Wooten's house, they parked a few doors down, and then they all hid there in the bushes. When Wooten came stumblin' home from the Mug-Shot Saloon and put his key in his front door, Levi whacked him in the head with his hockey stick, knockin' him unconscious. Todd and Levi dragged the Stupid Trooper inside, stripped him down to his underwear, and put him in bed. They unloaded his Trooper pistol and put the gun in his hand. Then Bristol and her best friend Angie (who were wearin' bikinis—thank goodness!) got into bed with Wooten, so Todd and Levi could snap off a whole bunch of incriminatin' pictures!

After Todd brought everyone back home, he raced off to my office, where he got the computer guy to hack into Wooten's Facebook page and load up all the photos!!!

This is even better than last year when Wooten was collectin' workers comp after he hurt his back from slippin' on ice, and then Todd started followin' him around to see if he was a phony baloney. Sure enough, Todd snapped pictures of Wooten huntin' and ridin' a snowmobile!!! Then he secretly gave those photos to Wooten's boss! I woulda loved to see the look on Wooten's face the day he got that letter cuttin' off his workers comp!

Dear Diary,

I can't believe I haven't heard a peep out of Monegan. What the heck is wrong with him?!? He must have seen those pictures of Wooten's Facebook page by now! Still, nothin'! What's it gonna take for Monegan to get the hint? This afternoon, Todd hopped in his Piper Cub, took to the skies, and wrote "Fire him!" in skywritin' over Monegan's house. C'mon, Monegan, get off your duff and do what needs to be done!

Dear Diary,

Enough is enough! I just couldn't take it anymore so I had my Chief of Staff Mike Tibbles fire Monegan—while I went out to the Beehive Beauty Shop for a pedicure. I told the press I wanna take the Department of Public Safety in a different direction, which is definitely true (THE DIRECTION OF FIRIN' MIKE WOOTEN!) I replaced Monegan with Chuck Kopp, who's been the Police Chief down there in the darlin' little town of Kenai. I picked Chuck Kopp not just because I fell madly in love with his name (Chuck Kopp. It's so manly. It sends chills up my spine. Chuck Kopp—Alaska's Top Cop! It sounds like a TV show!) but I chose him because he's a devoted Christian who was School Board President of a fundamentalist Christian high school and on the board of a bible camp, both founded by his father, who was a missionary. Anyone who loves Jesus as much as Chuck Kopp does will be overjoyed to do God's will and fire Wooten! After all, it's the Christian thing to do!

JULY 15, 2008

Dear Diary,

Todd sure did open a family-sized can of whoop-ass on the Stupid Trooper! He took Levi huntin' this afternoon. They shot a moose and threw it in the back of Todd's truck. Then, while Wooten was drinkin' at the Mug-Shot Saloon, they drove over to Wooten's house, chopped off the moose's head, and put it in Wooten's bed! It's just like Jesus said. If someone strikes ya on the right cheek, turn around and slap him right back.

Dear Diary,

    Yikes! That dog-gone Monegan is such a blabbermouth! He told the press that I fired his sorry keister all because he refused to fire Wooten. He said that me and Todd and folks in my administration kept pesterin' him with e-mails and phone calls about gettin' rid of Wooten. I was just tryin' to let him know that Wooten could be another Lee Harvey Oswald or Charlie Manson or Jeffrey Dahmer or O.J. Simpson or Hannibal Lecter.

    I can't believe Monegan said I have a vendetta against Wooten!!! That's just not true. I don't have a vendetta against him. He's just a beer-swillin', wife-cheatin', Taser-happy, gun-totin', white-trash freakazoid who shouldn't be a State Trooper, that's all. I've got nothin' personal against loserboy. And I certainly never put any pressure on Monegan to fire anybody. I just gave him a little encouragement, that's all. So what if I walked into his office one day, handed him an axe, and said, "Here, why dontcha give this to Wooten?" Or the time I walked into his office, handed him a boot, and suggested that he give it to the Stupid Trooper. C'mon Walt, where's your sense of humor? It was all

THE REAL REASON I FIRED WALT MONEGAN

1. HE REFUSED TO SHAVE OFF THAT SILLY MOUSTACHE (even though it makes him look like the guy on the box of Lipton Tea bags.)

2. HE WAS ALWAYS PLAYIN' SOLITAIRE ON HIS COMPUTER.

3. HE SPENT TOO MUCH TIME IN THE RESTROOM.

4. WHENEVER HE POURED THE LAST DROP OF COFFEE FROM THE COFFEE POT, HE NEVER MADE A NEW POT.

5. HE WORKED AGAINST THE INTERESTS OF THE PEOPLE OF ALASKA ON THE BUDGET (by tryin' to get more money for public safety).

6. I WANTED TO TAKE HIS DEPARTMENT IN A NEW DIRECTION — the same direction he was already takin' his department.

7. HE WASN'T DOIN' ENOUGH TO FILL STATE TROOPER VACANCIES. (He refused to hire unqualified people for the job.)

8. HE WASN'T A TEAM PLAYER (because he was too eager to be on a winnin' team).

9. HE WASN'T DOIN' ENOUGH TO COMBAT ALCOHOLISM IN RURAL AREAS. (So instead I offered him a job as head of the Alcohol Beverage Control Board.)

10. HE'S A BIG POO-POO HEAD.

in good fun! Well, I guess I better call Chuck
Kopp and tell him not to fire Wooten until this
Monegan thing blows over.

JULY 25, 2008

Dear Diary,

Holy mackerel! I can't believe this Monegan
situation just keeps gettin' worse! Chuck Kopp
resigned today, which makes me look like a real
twit for firin' Monegan and then hirin' that
pervert. Turns out Chuck Kopp received a letter
of reprimand for sexually harassin' a female
employee while he was Kenai Police Chief. Just
my luck. Now I gotta find another new Public
Safety Commissioner, like I've got nothin' else
to do! Well, on the bright side, when Monegan
finds out that I gave Chuck Kopp $10,000
in severance pay, he'll hit the ceiling. I gave
Monegan nothin'. Nyeh nyeh nyeh!!!

JULY 27, 2008

Dear Diary,

While the kids were playin' Monopoly, I
noticed that Levi has some kind of mark on his
ring finger. I grabbed his hand and took a closer
look. Yep, something was on his ring finger all
right. It was a tattoo of Bristol's name.

"What's that all about?" I asked.

Levi explained that Bristol had given him a promise ring, but he lost the ring while huntin' caribou, so instead of buyin' a new ring, he decided to get Bristol's name tattooed to his ring finger because he can't possibly lose a tattoo. Although in Levi's case, I think the boy is so dumb, he actually could lose a tattoo.

I just hope Bristol doesn't reciprocate by havin' her ring finger tattooed with the word "Dumbass."

MY FAMOUS MOOSE BURGER RECIPE

- SHOOT ONE MOOSE
- GRIND UP THE MEAT
- MAKE INTO PATTIES
- FLAME BROIL OVER BARBECUE

JULY 28, 2008

Dear Diary,

Snakes alive! I'm gettin' clobbered! Today the State Legislative Council voted unanimously to spend up to $100,000 to conduct an investigation to find out why I fired Monegan and whether I abused the power of my office. What a waste of taxpayer money! I mean, honestly! With that kind of money, we could toilet paper Wooten's house every day for the next ten years! Why am I the target? Wooten should be the target! I had my office issue a statement that I will cooperate fully with the investigation. Yeah, I'll cooperate fully all right. I'm happy to tell the world everything that my insane former brother-in-law did. This former beauty queen has nothing to hide. Well, nothing that a little makeup can't cover up.

July 31, 2008

Dear Diary,

Goodness gracious! Two of Alaska's Senators were in the news today! Too bad that darn Democratic State Senator Hollis French is such a pain in my rump roast! In today's WALL STREET JOURNAL, he said that I "could face impeachment, in a worst-case scenario." Impeachment?!? This is the guy in charge of my objective, unbiased, impartial investigation, and he's talkin' impeachment? How fair is this investigation gonna be? So, to keep things fair, I ordered my Attorney General, the ever-so-brilliant Talis Colberg, to conduct his own investigation. He didn't really wanna do it, but I told him that if he does, I'll read his dissertation on "M.D.

Snodgrass: The Founder of the Alaska State Fair." I betcha it's a real page-turner.

My good friend Republican Senator Ted Stevens was also in the news today, which was really exciting—except for the part about him being indicted on seven counts of corruption. But still, it's really cool turnin' on every news show to see the face of someone who endorsed me when I ran for Governor, appeared in a campaign commercial with me, and once appointed li'l ol' me as a director of a his 527 group. He's a real sweetie pie—for a corrupt, wrinkled old coot.

I was in the news, too, which was very cool. I did an interview on CNBC with Larry Kudlow, who said that I have a whole lotta fans who want me to be John McCain's Vice Presidential candidate. Why in the world would I ever wanna be Vice President? I mean, bein' Governor of Alaska is a super cool job that pays expenses for family trips. What's so cool about bein' Vice President? I mean, what exactly does the VP do every day besides sit around with a scowl on his face? Dick Cheney looks like a pretty miserable guy to me. I mean, the VP slot must be a pretty crummy job if he's such a sourpuss all the time.

THINGS TO DO

- BUY PAMPERS
- HIRE A NEW PUBLIC SAFETY COMMISSIONER
- MAKE AN APPOINTMENT FOR BRISTOL TO GET A SONOGRAM
- FIND OUT WHAT THE VICE PRESIDENT DOES

AUGUST 1, 2008

Dear Diary,

Heavens to Betsy! The Alaska Legislative Council named Stephen Branchflower (now what kind of sissy name is that?) as Special Counsel to investigate why I fired Monegan. I don't know much about this Branchflower fella, except that he used to be an assistant district attorney. I hear that he's a top-notch, respectable, heavy-duty prosecutor who can get to the bottom of this mess, for sure. I really don't know why they're going to all this trouble. I promised the Alaskan people that I'll cooperate with the investigation. I'm totally willin' to answer any questions anybody has about how Wooten cheated on my sister and tasered my ten-year-old nephew Payton. I better find out how my Attorney General is comin' along with our own little investigation so we can beat Branchflower to the punch. In the meantime, I've appointed a six-person committee to review candidates for Monegan's old job so I don't get caught with my pantsuit down again.

WHY I DON'T KNOW WHAT the VICE PRESIDENT'S JOB IS

* "The dog ate my copy of the U.S. Constitution."
* "Oh, Vice President! I thought you said Vice Principal."
* "They never really showed that on THE WEST WING."
* "Dick Cheney is in an undisclosed location and won't return my phone calls."
* "Of course I know what the Vice President does. I just can't tell you because it's a matter of national security."
* "I was briefed by Dan Quayle."

AUGUST 14, 2008

Dear Diary,

I think Talis Colberg's investigation is goin' just a little _too_ well. He discovered a tape recordin' of a phone call made by one of my staff members (that blabbermouth Frank Bailey!!!) to a State Trooper. Clear as day, Bailey tells the Trooper why Todd and I think that rootin' tootin' Wooten needs a bootin'. Talis played the tape for me, and I do have to say, Frank made some very persuasive talkin' points. But his getting caught on tape really makes me look bad. So I did what any self-respectin' person would do. I treated myself to a facial at the Beehive Beauty Shop.

Then I held a press conference to tell everyone about the Gotcha tape recording of Frank Bailey's phone call. I made it clear that I never asked Frank to make the call, which was just wrong. (Wrong of me not to ask him to make it!) I explained that my Attorney General Talis Colberg discovered that my staff, includin' Talis himself, made dozens of phone calls to Monegan's office, but no one was tryin' to pressure anyone to fire Wooten—except for Bailey whose phone call was totally improper (and the only one caught on tape, thank goodness).

I can see how Monegan might have interpreted all those phone calls as some kind of pressure (because it was), and I can see how all those phone calls might cause some folks to jump to the conclusion that I told my staff to make the calls (which would be accurate), but I can't see how a big lug like

Monegan could get all freaked out by a few petty phone calls. It's not like anyone called him up and just breathed heavily into the receiver (other than Todd and Levi).

REASONS WHY MY STAFF PHONED MONEGAN SO OFTEN

* THEY WERE ALWAYS INVITIN' HIM OUT TO LUNCH.
* THEY ALL HAD SECRET CRUSHES ON HIM.
* THEY WERE TRYIN' TO SELL HIM GIRL SCOUT COOKIES.
* WE WERE PLANNIN' A SURPRISE PARTY FOR HIM AND WE WERE TRYIN' TO THROW HIM OFF TRACK.
* HE WAS HAVIN' TROUBLE WITH HIS PHONE LINE AND WE WERE HELPIN' HIM TEST IT.
* HE TOLD US THAT THE 9TH CALLER WOULD WIN A FREE FISHIN' LICENSE.

AUGUST 19, 2008

Dear Diary,

When I got home from havin' my highlights done at the Beehive Beauty Shop, Todd told me that the Republican National Committee called to ask me if I would run for Vice President of the United States. That Todd! What a joker! I think a hockey puck must've hit him in the head!

MORE WAYS I CAN COOPERATE WITH THE INVESTIGATION

→ Call in a bomb threat to Branchflower's office from Wooten's cell phone.

→ Break into Branchflower's office and steal all the evidence.

→ Send my Attorney General Talis Colberg on a fact-findin' mission to Russia.

→ Put together a file of those photos from Wooten's Facebook page.

AUGUST 24, 2008

Dear Diary,

Jeepers, I can't believe it! Last night I got a phone call from Senator John McCain. He said he's considerin' me to be his runnin' mate.

"I'm very honored, Senator McCain," I said, "But I don't do any runnin'. I power walk. Maybe you should speak to my husband Todd. He's the athletic one in the family."

"You really are something, my friend," said Senator McCain. He explained that he wants me to be his Vice Presidential candidate.

"Well, what exactly does the VP do?" I asked.

"Oh, this and that," said McCain. He said he wanted to nominate Joe Lieberman as his runnin' mate, until he remembered that Lieberman is pro-choice. Havin' a Jew on the ticket is one thing, but it's something else to be runnin' for President with a Christ killer who woulda been happy to see Mary abort baby Jesus. That just makes me sick to my stomach.

"Well, if I'm gonna be VP, it's gotta be a heckuva lot cooler job than the one I have now, which I have to tell ya, is pretty gosh-darn cool," I said. "I just wanna make sure that if I'm movin' my entire family to Washington, D.C., that I'm doin' really cool stuff with lots of power and pizzazz."

I've only met McCain once . . . back in February at a meeting of the National Governors Association there in Washington, D.C. He looked much older in person. We chitchatted for a good fifteen minutes at the reception. He told me that his first wife Carol had been a swimsuit model and his second wife Cindy had been Junior Rodeo Queen there in Arizona, and then he asked me all about the swimsuit competition when I ran for Miss Alaska. He was tryin' his best to sneak a peek down my blouse, I'm sure, because I was six months pregnant and a cup size larger. He just seemed like a dirty old man to me.

On the phone he said, "Sarah, I see us workin' closely together, late into the night, if necessary, and I guarantee, my friend, that as my Vice President you'll have more access to the Oval Office than you ever dreamed possible."

Oh yuck! That's what I was afraid of. My mind flashed and I remembered hearin' how Nelson Rockefeller died while in a compromisin' position with his secretary on top of the desk there in his office, and suddenly I imagined McCain dyin' that same way, except the person in the compromisin' position was me, Sarah Palin, upstandin' hockey mom! Noooooo! But then it hit me! John McCain is more than just a dirty old man. He's a dirty old geezer who could croak any minute, and when he does, his Vice President will have the coolest job in the world, and that Vice President could be me!!! Me, me, me!!! So as Vice President I'd truly be a heartbeat away from the Presidency, which is soooo totally cool!

So I said yes, of course, and now all I do is picture the old geezer boinkin' his blond trophy wife Cindy on the desk in the Oval Office and havin' a heart attack. Todd says I'll be one boink away from the Presidency. That Todd!

When I got off the phone, Bristol came into my room to ask if she could try on some of my maternity clothes, and then I realized, oh boy, I probably oughta tell Senator McCain that my teenage daughter is pregnant and gonna have the baby. I have a feelin' that's not really gonna bode well. Bode. That's such a cool word. It'd make a great baby name. Well, before I tell McCain anything, I better make absolutely sure those two kids are really gonna tie the knot. But how am I ever gonna do that? Maybe Todd will have an idea that bodes well.

WHAT THE VICE PRESIDENT DOES

- Persuades the President to start wars
- Works behind closed doors with neo-con groups and oil companies to think up cool energy policies
- Declares "Executive Privilege" whenever Congress starts askin' nosy questions
- Lives in Vice President's residence—yeah!
- Obtains no-bid government contracts for family friends and fraternity brothers
- Operates all the paper shredders
- Hides out in an undisclosed secret location

Dear Diary,

I love my First Dude to pieces! He's so ingenious! He and Levi loaded up the truck with cans of glue and a bag of goose feathers. Todd said they were gonna go over to Mike Wooten's house, paint the glue on his bedroom walls, and then toss the goose feathers at the walls. Levi was totally psyched.

When they got to Wooten's house, they went inside, carryin' the cans of glue and bag of feathers, but when they closed the front door, Wooten jumped out from a closet and ambushed Levi, wrestlin' him to the floor and handcuffin' him to a chair!

Turns out, Todd had telephoned Wooten the day before and arranged the whole thing. He made a truce with Wooten in exchange for a little favor. Wooten hooked up his Taser to Levi usin' some wires with little clips, and then he asked Levi if he's really gonna marry Bristol.

"I think so," said Levi.

Wooten zapped him with the Taser for just a second, givin' him a little shock. Exactly what he did to my ten-year-old nephew Payton. Sort of like what it would feel like to touch an electrified fence. Todd said Levi's eyes bulged and he nearly leaped out of the chair, except he couldn't because he was handcuffed to it.

"So let me ask you again," said Wooten. "Are you really gonna marry Bristol?" He gave Levi another quick zap with the Taser.

"Y-y-y-yes, absolutely," stammered Levi.

"Are you sure now?" asked Wooten.

"Yes, definitely," said Levi. Todd told me the kid was scared to kingdom come.

"That's good," said Wooten. He took off the clips. "But just to make sure you don't forget..."

Wooten opened a can of glue and poured it all over Levi. Then Todd opened the bag of goose feathers and emptied it all over the kid. Can you imagine?!? Just picturin' Levi covered with feathers makes me laugh out loud. Todd threw Levi in the back of his truck and dropped him off in the parkin' lot of the high school, so the kid had to walk home all humiliated, lookin' like Big Bird!!! Gotcha!!!

AUGUST 27, 2008

Dear Diary,

This is so awesome! I'm on a plane for a top-secret meeting in Flagstaff, Arizona. I'm gonna rendezvous (that's spy talk for "meet up") with Senator McCain's top two aides.

We're gonna rendezvous at the home of some beer distributor who works for McCain's wife Cindy. I feel like I'm in a James Bond movie. I just love it!

I can't wait to tell them that today I signed a terrific bill to let TransCanada build a pipeline to send natural gas from the tippy top of Alaska down to the lower 48 states. This makes me the coolest Alaska Governor in history! People have been tryin' for 30 years to get this deal done, and I did it!!! This is so awesome! I totally rule!!!

It's a shame TransCanada doesn't have any natural gas to send through the pipeline. But that's not my problem! I'm sure the good folks at TransCanada can get BP, ConocoPhillips, and ExxonMobile to send their natural gas through the pipeline, once the muckety-mucks at those three oil companies get over not being a part of the pipeline deal. They're such sore losers. I can't believe BP and ConocoPhillips have teamed up to build their own pipeline. As if! They really need to get over themselves! That's why Alaska's future and America's security belongs in the hands of a Canadian company, by golly!

Todd tells me that the North Slope fields hold like 35 trillion cubic feet of natural gas, which he says is a lot, so I'm sure it is. Thank you God for blessin' me with a big handsome husband who works for BP in the oil fields and showed me how to fill the gas tank on a snowmobile (otherwise, I'd have no idea what I'm talkin' about). So now, if I've got this straight, Alaska gives $500 million to TransCanada to look into the possibility of investin' $27 billion of their own money to build the pipeline. If TransCanada doesn't build the pipeline, it's totally their fault, not mine. I still come out lookin' like a real go-getter for standin' up to the big oil companies and the good-ol'-boys — even if we don't get the $500 million back!!! I know in my heart that God is totally behind this project.

AUGUST 28, 2008

Dear Diary,

My rendezvous last night with McCain's aides went really well — even though I kept callin' Mark "Steve" and Steve "Mark" (Those two whipped up some tasty margaritas!!!), and

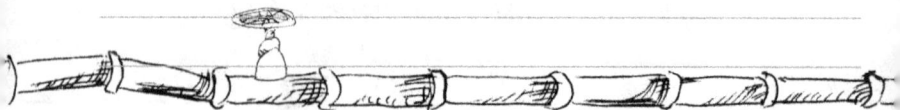

this morning, they drove me to the McCains' vacation home near Sedona, which I'm pretty sure is still there in Arizona. I had Steve and Mark blindfold me for the car ride because I just love feelin' like I'm in a James Bond movie. When we got to the house, the old geezer and his wife Cindy were lookin' pretty good (although Cindy did look a lot like a zombie), and we sat on the deck to chat.

Senator McCain told me to call him John, but I said I wasn't comfortable doin' that, so he asked me what I'd be comfortable callin' him.

"Gramps," I said.

"Okay, then Gramps it is," said McCain.

I'm glad he didn't ask me what I wanted to call Cindy, because I probably wouldn't have been able to stop myself from sayin' "The Ice Queen." I've seen ice sculptures at the Fairbanks Ice Festival with more warmth and personality than that Popsicle princess. She's a lot younger than the old geezer, so I didn't have any problem callin' her Mrs. McCain. The more I got to know her, the more she seemed like some sort of alien from that

movie INVASION OF THE BODY SNATCHERS. I really started to get the creeps when I realized how close we were to Roswell, New Mexico.

I had no idea until this morning what a chatterbox the old geezer is. He just droned on and on. He told me how he graduated 895th out of a class of 900 students from the United States Military Academy at Annapolis. He told me how he trained as a pilot at Naval Air Station Pensacola in Florida where he crashed his plane into Corpus Christi Bay. He told me how he was shot down over Vietnam and held as a prisoner of war at the Hanoi Hilton for more than five years. Bein' held prisoner in a five-star hotel with a swimmin' pool and room service sounded pretty nice to me, until the old geezer explained that the Hanoi Hilton wasn't a hotel at all. He told me how the Vietnamese had offered to release him early because his father was an Admiral, but he said "no thanks" because he preferred bein' tortured to goin' home to his wife. Blah, blah, blah, blah, blah. Cindy got so bored with the conversation that she excused herself and went back in the house.

"I never thought she'd leave," said McCain. Then he explained that when he did get home from Vietnam, he dumped his wife for Cindy, who was much younger and hotter, but that now that Cindy is gettin' old, he said he needed someone to "energize his campaign."

That was just the cue I needed. I stood up, took off my jacket, and tossed it on a chair. Then I unzipped my dress and let it drop to my feet. I was wearin' a hot red regulation one-piece Miss Alaska swimsuit. I started promenadin' across the deck to strut my stuff and show off my great poise.

"So whaddaya think, Gramps? Am I qualified to energize your campaign?"

"Well, my friend, you're the only potential candidate that I've met face-to-face," he said.

I kneeled down there in front of the old geezer and caressed his pant legs. "Well, then, how about if we go head-to-head?" I asked.

He said that would have to wait for a closed-door meeting, but that he could feel me energizin' the campaign already. "So how about it, Sarah? Would you like to join my ticket?"

"You betcha!" I said. I jumped to my feet and shook his hand. "It's a deal!"

"Okay, my friend," said Gramps, "but all this stays top secret until I make the announcement with you by my side tomorrow in Dayton, Ohio. Be sure to wear the swimsuit."

I thought he was bein' serious, but then he winked and said, "Gotcha!"

The next thing I knew I was bein' whooshed on a private jet with Mark, Steve, and more margaritas to Middletown, Ohio, where we checked into the Manchester Inn under fake names. This James Bond stuff is so much fun! Now I'm Mrs. Upton (hmm, Upton might be a pretty cool name for Bristol's baby), and I'm sittin' here in the Presidential Suite, just waitin' for Todd and the kids to knock at the door. The kids think they're comin' to Ohio to help celebrate our wedding anniversary, which luckily is tomorrow. Otherwise, they'd be text messagin' the secret to all their friends, because it really is _soooooo_ exciting! Goody goody gumdrops!!! I'm on my way to the White House, for sure! I tried to call my Mom and Dad to tell them the great news, but they were out huntin' caribou. Bummer!

AUGUST 29, 2008

Dear Diary,

Today was a triple celebration! Todd and I celebrated our 20th wedding anniversary, the old geezer celebrated his 72nd birthday, and at a campaign rally there in Dayton, Ohio,

Gramps announced me as his pick for his Vice President!!!! It was so exciting! There were more folks at that one rally than the entire population of Wasilla! It was unbelievable! They loved me! They really loved me!

Todd and I made Bristol carry baby Trig with a baby blanket over her belly to hide her bulge. It worked like a charm. No one could tell that Bristol is preggers, although at the end of the rally, she took away the blanket, and I overheard a Secret Service guy say into his walkie-talkie, "We've got a major development with the minor. The teen has shoplifted a watermelon."

It really didn't matter. Now that Gramps has told the world I'm his pick for VP, I can tell him that Bristol is pregnant. I mean, what's he gonna do about it now?

Besides, people really loved my speech! They went crazy! Gramps is totally against earmarks. So now that I'm a part of the Straight Talk Express, I'm totally against earmarks too. I told the crowd: "I've championed reform to end the abuses of earmark spendin' by Congress. In fact, I told Congress thanks, but no thanks, on that Bridge to Nowhere. If our state wanted a bridge, I said, we'd build it ourselves." They ate it up!

It's just like Joseph Goebbels said. "If you tell a big lie and repeat it again and again, people will believe you are tellin' the truth." Joseph Goebbels must have been a great American!

When the campaign rally ended, we all got aboard the Straight Talk Express, which is all about speakin' up for the rights of heterosexuals and protectin' the institution of marriage. And since we're ridin' the Straight Talk Express, that means Barack Obama must be ridin' the Gay Talk Express, with all the left-wing liberal gibberish about gay marriage.

Todd and I found Gramps and the Ice Queen there in the back of the bus. I said we had something important to tell him.

McCain looked really worried. "Bloggers on the Internet have been spreading wild rumors about you, my friend," he said. "They say you faked being pregnant with Trig to cover up the fact that Trig is actually Bristol's baby."

I started crackin' up. Todd did too. We couldn't stop laughin'.

"What's so funny?" asked McCain.

"There's no way on earth that Trig could be Bristol's baby," I said.

"Why is that?" asked McCain.

"Bristol's five months pregnant," I said.

BRIDGE TO NOWHERE

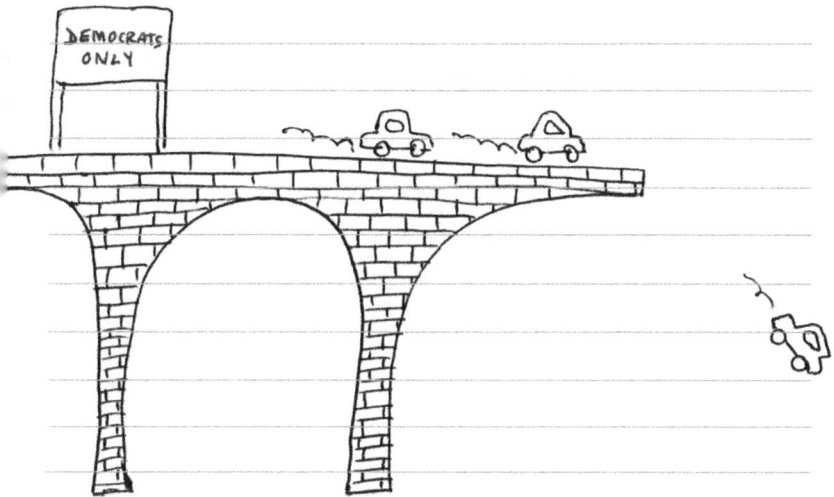

McCain burst out laughin', too. We were all in hysterics, except for Cindy McCain, who just sat there like a zombie, which made me laugh even harder. I've never laughed so hard in my entire life.

"That's great news," said McCain. "It totally kills the Internet rumors."

"Bristol's gonna have the baby and marry the father," I said.

"Fantastic," said McCain. "The Republican base will eat that up. You can't get more pro-life than that."

"And that's what the <u>Straight</u> Talk Express is all about," I said.

He said Bristol's baby will be "our little Battle of the Bulge" with the media. I guess he fought in the Battle of the Bulge durin' the Vietnam war.

But Gramps said we won't tell the media just yet. "First, we'll wait a few days to let America fall head over heels in love with Sarah Palin," he said, "just like I have."

Gramps picked up a remote control and pressed a button. A big flat-screen TV lowered down. He pressed another button to fire up the DVD player. "Have you ever seen the movie TOP GUN?" he asked. "It's all about this guy named Maverick."

"You betcha!" I said.

Todd and the kids really enjoyed watchin' the movie—especially in the middle of the movie when Gramps put on a pilot helmet printed with the name "MAVERICK" and danced down the aisle of the bus, singin' "Highway to the Danger Zone"! When the movie ended, Gramps yelled out, "Who wants to see it again?" And before anyone could answer, we were watchin' TOP GUN a second time. Something tells me this could be a very long campaign.

Dear Diary,

Ridin' aboard the Straight Talk Express has given Gramps and me time (in between watchin' Top Gun) to get to know how we each stand on the issues. Turns out Gramps thinks global warming is man-made. That's so ridiculous. The Republican Party platform may say global warming is man-made, but that doesn't make it true. Elitist scientists in their elitist laboratories may say global warming is man-made, but those are the same godless left-wing liberals who wanna teach our kids evolution and sex education. I know in my heart that God is the only one in control of the earth's thermostat. That's what makes me a maverick. But heck, I'm a team player, so from now on I'll just say no matter what's causin' global warming, we gotta do something about it (like pray).

Gramps also told me that he's against drillin' in the Arctic National Wildlife Refuge. That really shocked me. I mean, God put oil under the great state of Alaska because it's His will that we drill, baby, drill. But when Gramps put his hand on my knee, I got the strange feeling that he's tryin' to get me to drill, baby, drill in the Oval Office, before we drill, baby drill, in the Arctic National Wildlife Refuge.

I sure am amazed at how fast the McCain campaign gets things done. Lickety-split they removed the commercial showin' Senator Ted Stevens endorsin' me for Governor from my website. And when Gramps discovered that the TOP GUN disc was missin' from the DVD player (Todd secretly tossed it out the bus window!), I was amazed how quickly the campaign came up with another copy. I think they've got a whole box of backup TOP GUN DVDs hidden somewhere.

Tonight we had a big rally outside of Pittsburgh, so Bristol stayed on the bus to "baby-sit" Trig—to prepare for our sneak attack in the Battle of the Bulge.

AUGUST 31, 2008

Dear Diary,

Hurricane Gustav is about to hit New Orleans, so Gramps and I flew down to Jackson, Mississippi, to get a quick briefing on hurricane preparations to make sure President Bush doesn't botch this up again like he did with Hurricane Katrina. It breaks my heart to think that something as silly as a hurricane could destroy our chances of winnin' the White House, and I'm so sad that it's forced Gramps to scale back all those exciting plans for the Republication Convention. After an exhaustin' hour pretendin' that I care about the people of New Orleans and Mississippi, we flew to St. Louis for another big rally. We only got to watch the first half of TOP GUN on the plane ride down, so we watched the second half on the way to St. Louis. Gramps gave Todd and each of the kids a copy of TOP GUN for their flight back to Alaska, and he gave me a gift-wrapped copy of the deluxe edition for my flight to Minnesota and to give me inspiration while I'm waitin' for this guy named Scully to finish writin' my acceptance speech for the convention.

SEPTEMBER 1, 2008

Dear Diary,

Poor Bristol. Today she must have felt like JUNO in Juneau. My heart breaks for her. It really does. But she knew that Todd and I had to issue a statement to tell the world that she is five months pregnant and that she plans to marry Levi. It's the only way we could kill all those weird rumors bein' spread by those gosh-darn left-wing liberal bloggers that I faked bein' pregnant and pretended to give birth to Trig to cover-up the "fact" that he's actually Bristol's baby.

It really burns me up that Bristol has to deal with such a huge media storm on top of bein' a pregnant unwed teenager. When Todd and I eloped at the Palmer courthouse twenty years ago because I was a month pregnant with Track, we didn't have the added pressure of reporters and photographers and TV news crews wantin' to camp on our front doorstep. Bristol and Levi remind me of Todd and me at that age. We were high school sweethearts just like them. It bugs me that Levi dropped out of high school and quit the hockey team. But Todd was just as bad. He dropped out of college after takin' just a few courses, and when we were datin', he got arrested and taken to jail there in Dillingham for drunk drivin'. Well, Todd and I worked out just fine, so hopefully, Bristol and Levi will do okay, too.

I was holed up here in this fancy hotel room rehearsin' my acceptance speech, but my heart really ached for Bristol, and I really needed to cheer myself up. Normally, I'd go out, shoot a moose, grind it up into patties, and cook up some Moose Burgers, or dip 'em in chocolate and make Chocolate Moose. But there are no moose here in St. Paul (except at the zoo, which I don't think they'd take kindly to), but fortunately, one of the gals on the McCain Team told me to buy three suits for the convention and hire a stylist. She said a wealthy donor would be payin' for it all. So, lickety-split I called Neiman Marcus and made arrangements for them to open up the store after hours so I could do a little shoppin'.

The store gave me a personal shopper and together we found some really nifty designer outfits—gowns, jackets, pantsuits, dresses, blouses, shoes, and accessories. It was so much fun! I felt like Julia Roberts in PRETTY WOMAN tryin' on all these fabulous clothes! At the makeup counter, I hired my own personal stylist who gave me a great makeover. And I found some adorable dresses for the girls that I just couldn't resist, I got some really nice ties for Todd, and I picked out some luggage and an espresso maker. I was a little shocked when the bill came to $75,062.63, but heck, it's like my personal shopper said, if I wanna be elected Vice President, I can't go out there dressed like a hockey mom. I'm Caribou Barbie! I'm gonna shop till I drop!

Dear Diary,

I was cooped up here in this hotel room all day with nothing to do, so I turned on the TV to watch WHEEL OF FORTUNE, but all I could find was CNN. That no-good left-wing liberal press with their shameful Gotcha journalism! They had no right to dig into my past and report that as Mayor of Wasilla, I hired a lobbyist who got us almost $27 million in federal earmarks, which was really awesome at the time. (I'm one smart cookie, hiring a lobbyist who was the former Chief of Staff to Alaska Senator Ted Stevens, who just happened to be on the Senate Appropriations Committee that grants earmarks!)

I don't know how the WASHINGTON POST figured out that I requested $198 million in earmarks for the State of Alaska this year. Those big city reporters are devils, they really are! And those little devils dug up that when I ran for Governor, I supported the $223 million Bridge to Nowhere, but when the Bridge to Nowhere became a national joke, Congress cancelled it (and we got to keep the earmarked funds to pay for other things!!!). I'm just gonna ignore all that negativity and just keep repeatin'

WASILLA NEEDED EARMARKS TO:

- Buy new bowling balls for the North Bowl bowling alley
- Install arm-wrestling tables at the Mug-Shot Saloon
- Replace the dead fluorescent lights at the Wasilla Bible Church
- Build a shuffleboard court at the Lake Lucille Camping Park
- Subsidize construction of new Neiman Marcus and Sak's Fifth Avenue stores

that I'm against earmarks—just like that great American patriot Joseph Goebbels said to do.

That darn left-wing liberal press also figured out that Todd originally registered to vote as a member of the Alaskan Independence Party. I don't know why they're all bent out of shape just because the Alaska Independence Party wants to hold a vote on makin' Alaska its own country. I went with Todd to their annual convention in 1994 in Wasilla, and they were really a nice bunch of folks.

Todd, like most members of the Alaska Independence Party, joined because he thought he was registerin' independent. He had no idea that the party actually supports Alaskan independence. So, in 2002, Todd started all over again and registered as a genuine independent. I think a lot of folks register with the Alaskan Independence Party by mistake. I betcha that's why they're the third largest political party in Alaska. That's why, when I ran for Governor, I gave a speech at their convention. And this year, I recorded a video message for their convention. After all, if Alaska really does become its own country, that makes me President, and I'm all in favor of that!!!

Meanwhile, my lawyer came up with a really cool plan to deal with the Monegan investigation. He told the press that I have nothing to hide and I'm gonna cooperate fully with the investigation, and then he asked the Alaska Legislative Council to turn the whole investigation over to the State Personnel Board, which usually handles these sort of ethical inquiries. I thought that was so awesome! As Governor, I appointed the three members of the State Personnel Board, and I can fire them anytime I wanna—which would make this a fair investigation. When I saw Senator Hollis French say no, absolutely not, on CNN,

I wanted to take my shotgun and blast some holes in the TV, but I don't have my shotgun with me, so instead, I hurled the TV set out the hotel window so I could get to work rehearsin' my gosh-darn speech.

SEPTEMBER 3, 2008

Dear Diary,

Geeze Louise! I can't believe 37 million people watched me give my acceptance speech tonight at the Republican Convention on television! That's like a zillion more people than live in Alaska! Wow! I feel like a Republican rock star! Well, actually, bein' from Alaska, I guess that makes me the new Northern Star! Hahahaha! I crack myself up! It must be the champagne! What a crazy night! I'm the first woman to run for Vice President on the Republican ticket (darn those Democrats for beatin' me to the punch with Geraldine Ferrari!), and I heard people say I'm the first Alaskan to run for Vice President (I had no idea!), which is sooooo cool!

I was super busy all day rehearsin' my acceptance speech (with help, thank goodness, from Scully, who added a whole bunch of really great zingers), and I spent a lot of time pickin' out the right outfit to wear and gettin' my hair done, which really paid off big because the crowd went wild for me.

I was really touched today at the airport when Levi flew in with Todd and the kids, and they were all there to meet Gramps when he arrived at the airport. I don't know how Todd got Levi to get a haircut and shave and put on his Sunday best, but I have a sneaky feelin' Wooten mighta been involved. It was so sweet of Gramps to take Levi aside and give him a few words of wisdom ("Next time, use a condom!").

And when I was givin' my speech, it nearly brought tears to my eyes, lookin' up to see Levi sittin' next to Bristol hand in hand like two little lovebirds, and it was so nice that he came up to join our family on stage afterwards. Well, I gotta run, dear Diary. I hear Todd gettin' out of the shower, and I have a surprise celebration planned with a cute little outfit I found in the Neiman Marcus lingerie department!

SEPTEMBER 4, 2008

Dear Diary,

I don't read the NEW YORK TIMES because the type is too darn small, and they use too many twenty-dollar words, and I hear it's nothing but a bunch of godless left-wing liberal hogwash. But some people on the McCain Team told me that the NEW YORK TIMES reported that when I was Mayor of Wasilla, I tried to ban books from the public library, and that story was picked up by the ALASKA DAILY NEWS and it's goin' all over the Internet like wildfire.

I don't see what the big fuss is all about. All I did was ask our city librarian if she would be willin' to remove books from the library if I asked her to do so. I didn't name any books, but there are some pretty freaky books there in the library that teach kids about gay sex and stuff. The library lady flipped out and said she'd never agree to censorship. I wasn't talkin' about censorship, just gettin' rid of some weird books.

I thought her hairdo was just adorable, but I fired her because she wasn't a team player. Librarians are supposed to be sweet little things, not feisty bitches tryin' to pollute kids' minds with gay sex manuals and other left-wing liberal rubbish. I didn't expect folks there in town to protest like they did, so I decided to let the librarian keep her job so I wouldn't look like an ogre. No biggie. Instead, I just made her job miserable until she eventually quit.

Tonight Gramps made his big speech at the convention, goin' on and on about his bein' tortured as a POW and lovin' America, which brought tears to my eyes because I realized that over the next ten weeks I'm gonna have to listen to him tell that story again and again and again. Ughhh! I just loved when Gramps called himself a maverick, and I love bein' a maverick, too. When we were on stage at the end of the convention with our families, wavin' to the crowds of folks cheerin' and applaudin', with balloons fallin' and confetti flyin', Gramps leaned over and whispered in my ear that he felt just like Maverick in TOP GUN, and I smiled and gave him a wink and a big thumbs up, until I realized that makes me Goose.

SEPTEMBER 5, 2008

Dear Diary,

The old geezer's brain wasn't workin' very well today. While makin' a speech at our rally together here in Wisconsin, Gramps started talkin' about me and said, "She took the luxury jet that was acquired by her predecessor and sold it on eBay—and made a profit!" Yikes, he really made a mess-and-a-half of that.

I did put the jet up for sale on eBay (just

BOOKS I WOULD BAN AND WHY

If I had my druthers (whatever that means),
I'd burn these despicable books...

1. <u>HAMLET</u>. Hamlet's girlfriend is named
   Ophelia. That's just way too suggestive
   for this down-to-earth gal. I'm pretty
   sure Bristol was forced to read that
   in high school English class. It just
   obviously sends the wrong message.

2. <u>LEAVES OF GRASS</u>. Bill Clinton gave a
   bound copy of this book to Monica
   Lewinsky. That says it all to me. It
   must be obscene. I don't care if Walt
   Whitman does make those delicious
   chocolate samplers. Give a young girl
   chocolates, not an X-rated poetry book.

3. <u>LYSISTRATA</u> by Aristophanes. In this
   ancient Greek play, the women stop
   havin' sex with their husbands until
   the men agree to use mouthwash.
   Innocent kids get lured into readin'
   this rubbish because from the title
   they think it's about fightin' plaque.

4. <u>OEDIPUS REX</u> by Sophocles. A guy kills
   his father and marries his mother. ➡

Ewwwww!!!!! Gross!!!! This sounds worse than *DESPERATE HOUSEWIVES*! No wonder the word "sophomoric" comes from Sophocles.

5. *ORIGIN OF SPECIES* by Charles Darwin. This book is a pack of left-wing liberal lies. Evolution, schmevolution! Everyone knows the world was created in six days. The Bible tells me so!!!

6. *THE ADVENTURES OF HUCKELBERRY FINN.* Samuel Clemens wrote this book under the pen name Mark Twain. Why didn't he use his real name? What did he have to hide? I bet he was Jewish.

7. *HARRY POTTER.* These anti-Christian books promote witchcraft, wizards, demons, and the occult. They're the devil's work to get kids to fall under Satan's evil spell. And they're way too long.

8. *THE NEW YORK TIMES.* I know it's not a book, but if that newspaper is gonna write mean stories about me, then they (along with the *WASHINGTON POST* and the *BOSTON GLOBE*) are nothing but kindling for my fireplace!

like I promised I would durin' my campaign for Governor), but there was only one serious bid—wouldn't ya know it?—and unfortunately, it fell through. Fiddlesticks!!! So instead, Johnny Harris, the Republican Speaker of the Alaska House, brokered a deal and sold the plane to an Alaska businessman for $2.1 million. A heck of a lot of money, sure, but the State of Alaska originally bought the plane for $2.7 million. So we didn't exactly make a profit, like Gramps said. But that's okay. Larry Reynolds, the guy who bought the plane, contributed to my campaign in 2006 and to Johnny's campaign in 2007, so who knows? Maybe I really did make a profit like Gramps said.

Dear Diary,

I'm sorry I haven't had any time to write, but the campaign has been really hectic! It's crazy! I've got my own campaign RV called the No Talk Express because it's set up like a big classroom on wheels, and my prep team doesn't want me doin' any interviews with the press until they've finished with our tutorin' sessions. I feel like I'm in the movie MISS CONGENIALITY in that scene where Michael

Caine coaches Sandra Bullock on how to be a beauty contestant, except I don't need any coachin' in that department because I know my stuff when it comes to pageant walkin', poise and bearin', the talent portion, and the swimsuit competition. We're just focusin' on the Onstage Question and it's just non-stop crammin'.

Different folks hop on and off the RV to tutor me for an hour here or a half-hour there, and they keep givin' me all these serious books and briefin' materials and thick notebooks filled with all sorts of stuff. There are so many different experts tryin' to teach me stuff, I can't keep their names straight, so I just call each one of them Professor and give 'em a wink, which makes them feel really important and special. I feel like I'm back in college crammin' for final exams. I really do.

There's no way on God's good earth I'm ever gonna read all this junk, so I just ask them to summarize it for me or give me CLIFFS NOTES or put together some flash cards. I also got them to make up some flash cards for Willow and help her study for her Social Studies class. She's got a big test coming up on the names of all the U.S. Presidents.

All this coachin' and studyin' and quizzin' between campaign rallies is really exhaustin'. We've been crisscrossin' the country, goin' from Michigan to Colorado to New Mexico to Missouri, then back to Ohio and Pennsylvania, givin' the same speeches. I just wish I could get off the RV somewhere and pick up some new outfits at Saks Fifth Avenue or Bloomingdale's, but there just hasn't been any time. I never thought I'd ever say this, but I'd be happy just to kick back with a six-pack and watch TOP GUN.

Speakin' of TOP GUN, I think Gramps might be takin' that movie way too seriously. On Saturday night, we flew together on the campaign jet from Michigan to Colorado. I was sittin' at a table there in the back gettin' quizzed on the names of leaders of the Arab countries (they're so hard to pronounce!), and Gramps was sittin' ahead of me wearin' his "MAVERICK" pilot helmet and watchin' TOP GUN for the umpteenth time, when suddenly Gramps danced his way up the aisle to the cockpit and convinced the pilot to let him fly the plane for a little while. He really thinks he's Maverick from the movie! Suddenly the song "Highway to the Danger Zone" was blastin' over the sound system, and Gramps made an announcement for us to buckle our seatbelts, and the plane broke into rollovers and loop-de-loops and nosedives. I had no idea until that moment that the campaign actually printed up official McCain-Palin barf bags.

Dear Diary,

That gosh-darn WASHINGTON POST is really startin' to fry my bacon. Today those left-wing troublemakers reported that as Governor, I charged the State of Alaska for travel expenses while livin' at home there in Wasilla for 312 nights — as if that's some sort of crime, which it's not! They just don't understand that as Governor I'm entitled to a "per diem" of $60 a day for food and incidental expenses while travelin' on state business, and since my office is officially 600 miles away there in Juneau, livin' at home and commutin' 45 miles to my Anchorage office qualifies as travelin' on state business. I know that sounds ridiculous, but that's what a maverick does, by golly!

Besides, I've saved Alaska tons of money by flyin' coach, sellin' the state jet, drivin' myself to work, gettin' rid of the chef at the

HOW TO SPEAK MAVERICK

Words Mavericks Use

* **MAVERICKING**—to participate in maverick activities. "If anyone calls, tell them I'm out mavericking."

* **MAVERICKED**—feelin' like a maverick. "This situation has me totally mavericked up!"

* **MAVERICKOCISM**—a witty remark that only a maverick would say. "Everything Sarah Palin says is a maverickocism."

* **MAVERICKOLOGY**—the study of mavericks. "You don't need a degree in Maverickology to know I'm a maverick."

* **MAVERICESS**—a maverick princess. "Presentin' her royal Mavericess, President Sarah Palin!"

* **MAVERICKNESS**—that special quality that makes someone a maverick. "Sarah Palin was born with maverickness."

* **MAVERICKALITY**—the unique personality of a maverick. "The Governor of Alaska has such a dynamic maverickality."

* **MAVERICKOSITY**—possessin' the special traits of a maverick. "Her maverickosity endeared Governor Palin to Americans." →

* MAVERICIZE—to turn a non-maverick into a maverick. "When I get into the White House, I'm gonna mavericize Congress!"

* MAVERICATE—to force mavericky ideas upon a non-maverick. "I'm gonna mavericate until those left-wing liberal do-nothings see things my way."

* MAVERICKOWITZ—a Jewish maverick. "That Joe Lieberman is such a maverickowitz!"

* MAVERICKABLE—able to be changed into something a maverick would like. "Is that economic stimulus plan maverickable?"

* MAVERICKABILITY—the ability to act like a maverick. "That Barack Obama really lacks maverikability."

* MAVERICKESQUE—to be stylish like a maverick. "Sarah Palin's wardrobe is exceptionally maverickesque."

* MAVERIFIC—supremely unique. "Governor Palin made a maverific speech."

* MAVERICKOSEXUAL—to be sexually attracted to mavericks. "Todd and I are obviously maverickosexuals."

Governor's Mansion there in Juneau, and buyin' my pantyhose at Target!!! Everyone's gettin' all bent out of shape because the State of Alaska reimbursed me $17,059?!?!? What's the big deal? I spent more than that for a couple of jackets and skirts at Saks Fifth Avenue!!!

SEPTEMBER 11, 2008

Dear Diary,

Last night, I flew back here to Alaska for a few days, with a prep team (Doug, Steve, and Randy — gotta remember those boys' names!) to coach me for my big ABC-TV interview with Charlie Gibson. I really wanted to ask Charlie Gibson if he's related to Mel Gibson. I love his movie THE PASSION OF THE CHRIST and how he gave that cop who pulled him over a piece of his mind. I'd like to get Mel to help me deal with the Stupid Trooper. But the boys said that might not be a great idea. Party poopers!

Finally, I told them that they don't have to treat me like Sandra Bullock in the movie MISS CONGENIALITY, because I actually won the Miss Wasilla Pageant, and when I came in runner-up in the 1984 Miss Alaska Pageant, I was awarded the title of Miss Congeniality. Doug, Steve, and Randy were actin' like such know-it-alls just because they have all sorts of Washington experience and diplomas from fancy-schmancy schools like Princeton and whatever. So, I had to put my foot down and let them know that hey, this candidate for VP went to Hawaii Pacific College, transferred to North Idaho Community College, transferred again to the University of Idaho, won a scholarship from the Wasilla beauty pageant to transfer to Matnuska-Sustina Community College, and then transferred back to the University of Idaho where I graduated with a bachelor's degree in communications/journalism, which means I can definitely spell the word "potato." I let them know that I've worked as a television sports reporter, so I know how to handle myself on TV. I'm the youngest Governor and the first woman Governor in Alaskan history. They don't call me Sarah Barracuda for nothing!

I think my interview with Charlie Gibson rocked! When he asked me if I agree with the Bush Doctrine, I thought, uh-oh, I shoulda studied that one. No one told me that was gonna be on the test. I wanted to say, "You're not a game show host, Charlie. This isn't ARE YOU SMARTER THAN A FIFTH GRADER?" Although I really wish I coulda used a Lifeline and called a

What the Bush Doctrine Is

* SHOCK AND AWE
* CAPTURIN' OSAMA BIN LADEN DEAD OR ALIVE
* HOLDIN' HANDS WITH PRINCE ABDULLAH
* DEMANDIN' THAT THE PEOPLE'S REPUBLIC OF CHINA "TEAR DOWN THIS WALL!"
* WHATEVER DICK CHENEY SAYS IT IS
* "BROWNIE, YOU'RE DOIN' A HECK OF A JOB!"

friend. So, I just carefully danced around that one, bein' really, really vague, until I got Charlie to spell out for me what the Bush Doctrine is. I don't think anyone watchin' could tell that I had no idea what I was talkin' about. But honestly, why should anyone be expected to know what the Bush Doctrine is? I betcha George W. Bush doesn't even know what the Bush Doctrine is. Why dontcha ask me about something Americans really care about, like Monster Truck rallies, or who won the latest NASCAR race, or how late is Wal-Mart open? Aside from that little hiccup (which I'm sure no one noticed), I totally nailed that interview.

This afternoon was really emotional for me. I gave a farewell speech at Ft. Wainwright to send my first-born child off to Iraq. It's hard to believe that Track is off to Iraq. I love the way that rhymes. Track is off to Iraq to eat a Big Mac. I'm just so proud of Track and so relieved to know he won't be hangin' around the house — smokin' weed, binge drinkin', or snortin' Oxycontin. Hit the road, Track!

SEPTEMBER 13, 2008

Dear Diary,

Things are gettin' way out of hand! The Alaska Legislative Council issued subpoenas for 13 witnesses, includin' Todd (yikes!), in the Troopergate investigation. Fortunately, they didn't issue a subpoena for me — since that would look super bad. I just want this Troopergate investigation to disappear like the Arctic ice shelf.

I really hate how the press keeps callin' this mess "Troopergate," as if this is some kind of Watergate or Monicagate scandal that's gonna bring down my governorship or governorhood (or whatever it's called!) Man, oh man, that's not good at all. "Troopergate" makes me sound guilty of abusin' the power of my office. We need a better name for it. Something that doesn't sound so negative against me. Something that points the

finger back at Wooten. He's the one who tasered
my ten-year-old nephew Payton.

BETTER NAMES FOR
TROOPERGATE

* Wootengate
* Stupidgate
* Drunkengate
* Paytongate
* Wasillagate
* Tasergate ✓
* Trailertrashgate
* Whitetrashgate

Yeah, that's it. From now on, I'm callin' this
incident "Tasergate." That'll get folks pointin'
their fingers at Wooten, instead of me and Todd.

SEPTEMBER 14, 2008

Dear Diary,

This is so cool! Last night on SATURDAY
NIGHT LIVE, Tina Fey pretended to be me,
standin' alongside some other actress on the
show pretendin' to be Hillary Clinton. Wow!
If SATURDAY NIGHT LIVE is makin' fun of me, I
must be really famous! This is just incredible!
Two years ago I was Mayor of Wasilla, and
now, shazam! — I'm homecoming queen! It's
amazin' how much Tina Fey looks like me. She's
really beautiful! I thought she did a great
job, until I spoke with Bristol on the phone

who said Tina Fey was makin' fun of me — and Levi and his hockey buddies thought it was hysterical. Hmmm. Todd said he can put an end to Tina Fey's impersonation of me, if I want. All I gotta do is say the word. I just don't know what word he's talkin' about.

SEPTEMBER 16, 2008

Dear Diary,

Gramps hired a real tough lawyer (I call him "Slick") to help my attorney in Alaska (Slick calls him "Moose") put an end to the ~~Troopergate~~ Tasergate investigation or at least postpone it until after the election. Slick really knows how to shake things up. He told reporters that I'm unlikely to cooperate with the Alaskan Legislative inquiry because things have gotten way too political — since Democratic Senator Holis French is runnin' this investigation like a gosh-darn witch hunt. Then Slick and Moose filed a new motion with the Personnel Board. They wanna dismiss Moose's previous request for an ethics inquiry, because there's "no probable cause" to go after me, whatever that means. I love how those two legal mavericks are really rufflin' some feathers.

AMERICA AS I SEE IT

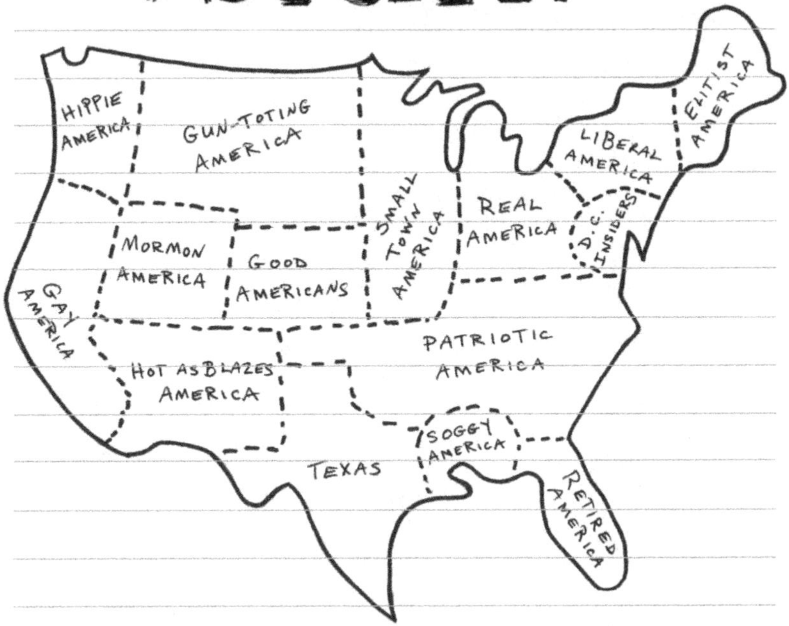
HIPPIE AMERICA
GUN-TOTING AMERICA
ELITIST AMERICA
LIBERAL AMERICA
SMALL TOWN AMERICA
REAL AMERICA
D.C. INSIDERS
MORMON AMERICA
GOOD AMERICANS
GAY AMERICA
PATRIOTIC AMERICA
HOT AS BLAZES AMERICA
SOGGY AMERICA
TEXAS
RETIRED AMERICA

SEPTEMBER 17, 2008

Dear Diary,

That Sean Hannity is a real sweetheart. Doin' a television interview with him was easy as pie. He wasn't tryin' to catch me off guard or stump me like I was takin' some sort of final exam. Instead, he tossed those softballs right over the plate so I could take whacks at Barack Obama (which Sean just loved) and talk about all the ways I'm gonna ruffle feathers and reform reform reform, and he never seemed to mind if I changed the subject without ever answerin' the question—because he's a maverick himself and such a cutie pie.

Tonight, I took part in my first town-hall meeting with Gramps. I felt right at home at Grand Rapids Community College. I really did. The people were really nice, and no one tried to play Stump-the-Candidate—even though I was ready for 'em. I practiced with my flash cards all day. The 7th President of the United States? Andrew Jackson. The capital of Uzbekistan? Tashkent. The 20th President? John Garfield. The capital of Botswana? Who the heck cares? Thank you! Thank you very much!

Dear Diary,

Todd is so brave! I just love him to pieces! He ripped up his subpoena and refused to show up in court to testify about his role in the ~~Troopergate~~ Tasergate investigation—even though he could be fined and sentenced up to six months in jail! He's such a dreamboat!!! So are all the other folks from my office who were slapped with subpoenas and refused to cooperate. Now all their names are bein' sent to the Alaska Senate on contempt charges. It sounds awful, but the Alaska Senate doesn't meet again until January, so they can't vote on the contempt charges until after the election! So even if Todd does get sentenced to jail time, it won't be until after the election and after Bristol's baby is born! Hip, hip, hooray!!! Saved by the bell!!!

Dear Diary,

Golly-gosh-a-mighty! The Lord blessed me with an awesome day! When it comes to foreign policy experience, I'm no dummy. I've had a passport for a year now, so I know my stuff. But today my prep team gave me an amazin' crash course on foreign policy! I learned so much!!! Never in a million, gazillion years did I ever think that I'd spend more than an hour alone there in a room with Henry Kissinger! I'm not really sure who Henry Kissinger is, which is why I never thought I'd ever spend an hour alone with him. We met there in his Park Avenue office, and he briefed me on something, I'm still not sure what exactly, because I couldn't understand a word he said. He just mumbles in this really thick accent, so I just nodded and smiled and winked and pretended I was really interested in whatever he was sayin'. His office is filled with books, but I betcha he hasn't read any of them. He probably just keeps them on his shelves to impress folks, the same way I do. He did mumble something about bein' glad Gramps has taken a tough stand against Russia for invadin' Georgia. Well, of course, we can't just let Russia take over Georgia. Next thing ya know they'll invade South Carolina and Alabama.

I also got to talk with Afghan President Hamid Karzai, who was stayin' at the Hotel InterContinental, and I asked him how he liked the hotel, if it has a good gym, whether he's ever tried a Stairmaster, if he's used the Jacuzzi. He said the hotel doesn't have a Jacuzzi, but he gave me a really nice tour of the mini-bar there in his room, and he let me feel how plush the bathrobes are.

I also met with Colombian President Alvaro Uribe, who served me the most delicious cup of coffee I've ever had. I asked him if he knew Juan Valdez, but he explained that Juan Valdez is a made-up character created by an advertising agency and played by an actor in the commercials, which broke my heart. He was curious how my tutorin' was goin', so I told him exactly what my prep team trained me to

say: "The rain in Spain falls mainly on the plain."
I love how that rhymes. It's just like "Track is
off to Iraq to eat a Big Mac."

Reporters are dyin' to interview me, and
they're really startin' to go stir crazy because
my prep team is holdin' them back. Those
reporters are like sled dogs just itchin' to get
out on the snow and run. Actually, they're
really more like a pack of wild wolves that
wanna sink their teeth into me and rip me apart.
So, I'm gettin' plenty of target practice first.

SEPTEMBER 24, 2008

Dear Diary,

I really beefed up my foreign policy know-
how today! Let's see. First, Gramps and I met
with President Mikheil Saakashvili of Georgia
(a foreign country near Russia, not a state like
I thought, which explains why Jimmy Carter
was such an awful President!!!) and President
Viktor Yushchenko of Ukraine (I just called
him Vic). Those guys have such crazy names!
And speakin' of crazy names, I had a private
meeting with Jalal Talabani, the President of
Iraq. I don't understand why his last name is
Talabani. Aren't we fightin' against the Taliban
there in Afghanistan? So why is the Taliban

President of Iraq? That just doesn't make any sense to me. I didn't say anything because I'm sure President Bush knows what he's doin', so I asked Talabani to keep an eye on Track and make sure he stays out of trouble. He promised to invite Track to the palace for some Moose Burgers so Track won't get homesick. What a sweetheart!

I also met with President Asif Ali Zardari of Pakistan (Ewww! What a lech!) and Prime Minister Manmohan Singh of India (wears a sheet wrapped around his head for some reason). Meetin' with all these weirdos made me realize that we're the only country on earth that hasn't switched to the metric system. That's because we're a country of mavericks! We stick to our guns, by golly.

But then I realized that we could solve a whole lot of problems facin' America by just switchin' to the metric system. For instance, if you're drivin' the speed limit, you can go 60 miles per hour. But if we switched to the metric system, you could go 100!!! For the price of one gallon of gas, you could buy _four_ liters!!! That's four times as much! Say the temperature outside is 80 degrees Fahrenheit. If we switch to Celsius, the temperature

drops to 27 degrees! It ends global warming!
Problem solved! Obesity is another huge
problem facin' America. But if we switch to
the metric system, instead of weighin' 200
pounds, you only weigh 90 kilograms! I think
this will really shake things up!

I did an interview with Katie Couric for
the CBS EVENING NEWS, which went really well.
She's a perky little ball-buster, that one, but
if I didn't know the answer to something, I
just strung together a bunch of the talkin'
points I memorized and then I just started
talkin' in tongues like folks used to do back
at the Wasilla Assembly of God and I threw
in some buzzwords like "health care reform,"
"job creation," and "shorin' up our economy,"
and she bought the snow job—hook, line, and
sinker. And if she really tried to pin me down
on something, I just said, "hey, I'll have to get
back to ya on that one," which worked like a
charm, just like when I was Mayor of Wasilla.

SEPTEMBER 25, 2008

Dear Diary,

Well, Gramps suspended our campaign so he
could put on his "MAVERICK" pilot helmet and do
a few barrel rolls over the Capitol building as

he flew back to Washington, D.C. to fix the economy. Goodness gracious! I can't believe our economy is on the brink of disaster! It breaks my heart. It really does. But I gotta tell ya, I know exactly why the economy is in such a mess.

George Washington's picture is on the $1 bill because he's our first President, which makes perfect sense. But George Washington's picture is also on the quarter. That's _sooooo_ ridiculous! It should be on the penny. But on the penny is a picture of Abraham Lincoln, whose picture is also on the $5 bill. Lincoln's picture should also be on the nickel, gosh darn it. But on the nickel is a picture of Thomas Jefferson, whose picture is also on the $2 bill—even though he was our third President! Everything is topsy-turvy!

That's why the economy is in such a pickle. If we really wanna straighten out the economy, we have to straighten out the money!

Abraham Lincoln's picture shouldn't be on the $5 bill. He was our sixteenth President! On the $5 bill should be a picture of our fifth President, James Monroe, whose picture should also be on the nickel. C'mon, America, that's a no-brainer!

On the $10 bill is a picture of Alexander Hamilton, who was never President of the United Sates. That's just wrong! If you ain't been President, you shouldn't get your picture on the money!

On the $10 bill should be a picture of our tenth President, John Tyler, who I just love! He was the first Vice President to become President, after William Henry Harrison, who was President for just one month. Harrison died from pneumonia because he didn't wear a coat to his inauguration. (NOTE TO SELF: Tell Gramps how handsome he looks without a coat.)

Tyler should also be on the dime. But who's on the dime? Franklin D. Roosevelt, who was our 32nd President. That's pretty insultin' to FDR, even if he was a Democrat. The dime is smaller than the nickel and smaller than the penny. This is why our economy is teeterin' on the brink of disaster.

So the dime should be the penny, the penny should be the nickel, and the nickel should be the dime. And instead of havin' George Washington's picture on the quarter, we should have a picture of our 25th President, William McKinley—with a picture of Alaska's Mt. McKinley on the back! That would rock!!!

On the $20 bill, we've got Andrew Jackson, who was our 7th President. It's just crazy! Instead, we should have our 20th President— John Garfield (I really nailed those flash cards!) And the $50 bill has a picture of Ulysses S. Grant, who was our 18th President. That doesn't make any sense! We haven't even had a fiftieth President! So there shouldn't be a $50 bill! When Gramps kicks the bucket and I become the 45th President, we can put a picture of me on a $45 bill, and combined with James Monroe on a $5 bill—presto!—you've got $50.

The $100 bill has a picture of Benjamin Franklin, who was never President! All he did was go out and fly a kite in a lightnin' storm. He coulda been killed. Is this who we want as a role model for our children? I don't think so! We might as well have Evil Kneival on the $100 bill.

But I know just how to solve this problem and energize the economy. I'm not a maverick for nothing! When I become President, I'll get the Treasury Department to Photoshop a picture of John Tyler (#10) in between two pictures of me (#45). That adds up to 100!

Now that's what I call an economic stimulus plan!

Dear Diary,

That gosh-darn elitist Gotcha Media is swarmin' like flies to a dead moose. Katie Couric showed some of our interview last night on the CBS EVENING NEWS, and now the media is gettin' in a tizzy because I said Vladimir Putin sometimes rears his head into Alaskan airspace. How was I supposed to know that neither Putin nor any Russian warplanes have flown into airspace over Alaska since I've been Governor? But that's not the point. They could do that anytime they feel like it. Even if they don't, I know for a fact that Santa Claus flies into Alaskan airspace every Christmas Eve on his way to the lower 48 states. Alaska is really close to the North Pole. I bet from the tippy top of Alaska you can see Santa's workshop. Plus, we've got Canada right on our border, and you really have to watch out for those Canadians. I've done everything in my power as Governor to stop those useless Canadian coins from gettin' into our country! That's what I call international experience, baby!

The media elite with their fancy-pants diplomas from those snooty New England colleges are just jealous of this no-nonsense hockey mom because they don't think an average person has what it takes to be President. They forget that Abraham Lincoln never went to college. Neither did Harry S Truman. In fact, Harry S Truman didn't even have an actual middle name. The S didn't stand for anything. He didn't even have a period after it. How weird is that? That's just un-American.

I don't trust people who use the first initial of their first name either. Like L. Frank Baum, the author of THE WIZARD OF OZ. What was he tryin' to hide? Turns out his first name was Lyman. I looked that up on Wikipedia. You can learn a lot of fascinatin' things on the Internet. F. Scott Fitzgerald. There's another one for ya. Well, I just entered his name, and turns out the F stands for Francis. Who woulda thunk? And J.K. Rowling, who wrote those satanic HARRY POTTER books with all that yucky wizardry and witchcraft. Her name is Joanne Kathleen. Why is she hidin' that? She's got some kind of pact with the devil, if ya ask me.

Well, all I gotta say is: this moose-huntin' hockey mom is super qualified to be President. You're darn tootin'! If I can balance bringin' one kid to the emergency room with a broken nose, gettin' in my hours at the Snack Shack, and keepin' my teenage daughter away from the boys and Oxycontin, surely I can run the country. How hard can it be? I mean, honestly. But those godless left-wing liberals there in the media keep sayin' that I haven't been properly vetted. I'm not a dog or a horse. I don't need to see a vet. Besides, Gramps is a Vietnam vet, so that should count for something.

Of course, not everyone there in the Gotcha Media is an evil sinner. There are plenty of sweethearts. Like Hugh Hefner. I was so flattered today when he invited me to pose in PLAYBOY if I'm not elected Vice President. Of course, I'd never do it (because it would freak out the kids and Todd would throw a fit) but that would be such an amazin' way to kick-off my campaign for President in 2012—especially if I was Miss November.

TURN-ONS: Huntin', Drillin', Snowmobilin', Creationism, Jesus, Speakin' in Tongues, Abstinence, Shopping Sprees, Free Grand Slam Breakfast at Denny's.

TURN-OFFS: Washington Insiders, Stem Cell Research, Abortion, Sex Education, Evolution, the Gotcha Media!!!

Dear Diary,

   Hot diggety dog! I'm havin' so much fun at Debate Camp, hunkered down here in this swank Four Seasons Hotel in Philadelphia, sharin' a room with Willow so she can be with me on the campaign trail. We're such great roommates! Last night we popped up some popcorn to watch Gramps debate Barack Obama, but it was really pretty boring, so after ten minutes, we changed the channel and watched HANNAH MONTANA and a whole bunch of other shows on the Disney Channel instead. It was like havin' our own private slumber party!

   My prep team has me memorize all sorts of talkin' points, and then I stand behind a podium and debate someone pretendin' to be Joe Biden, and I just string together my talkin' points and it's a hoot! I'm really havin' a blast! I haven't told them yet, but for the talent portion, I'd really like to put on an Alaska State Trooper uniform and sing my version of the ABBA song "Super Trouper"! I haven't brought up the idea yet because my prep team is gettin' really grouchy!!! They say when I string the talkin' points together they're comin' out of my mouth like a blizzard of words, as if this

Alaskan gal doesn't know how to snow shoe through a blizzard.

"Look, I was captain and point guard of the Wasilla High School basketball team," I said. "I know how to play defense." And I know how to practice! So tonight, Willow and I snuck down to the prep room here in the hotel, and I had Willow stand on a chair behind one podium and I stood behind the other, and we practiced debatin'—with Willow pretendin' to be Joe Biden. She may only be 13 years old, but she's sharp as a whip. It's just like when I help her with current events for her social studies homework, except now she's helpin' me. She's much more fun than any of those cranky fuss-budgets on my prep team, and she loves when I string together those talkin' points! It's gonna be a piece of cake to beat Joe Biden. Those hair plugs can't possibly compete with my legs, a push-up Wonderbra, and pink lip gloss.

SEPTEMBER 28, 2008

Dear Diary,

Tina Fey must die!!!! Now I know where that bitch (pardon my escargot) got the inspiration to write the movie MEAN GIRLS. From herself! Sheesh! I can't believe she made so much fun of my interview with Katie Couric! Willow thought it was hysterical, which really burns me up. When I become Vice President, my first order of business will be to replace SATURDAY NIGHT LIVE. We desperately need more wholesome TV shows for our children. I'm gonna issue an executive order to force those gosh-darn network executives to produce good, clean shows like . . . .

MY IDEAS FOR FAMILY TV SHOWS

- "PARENTAL NOTIFICATION!" In this pro-family show, hidden cameras zoom in on parents as they get notified that their underage daughter wants an abortion.

- "ALASKAN IDOL!" A show dedicated to the Miss Alaska Beauty Pageant with plenty of action behind the scenes.

- "SHOOT THAT WOLF!" Alaskan hunters compete for prizes as they fly in private planes to shoot as many wolves as possible.

- "WHAT'S MY ZIP CODE?" On this game show, a panel of judges guess the contestant's five-digit Zip Code.

- THE IDITAROD CHANNEL. An entire channel devoted to dog sled racin' and the Iditarod Trail—just for Todd and all his buddies.

Dear Diary,

I'm so glad that Gramps moved my Debate Camp from that stressed out Four Seasons Hotel there in Philadelphia to his vacation home here in Arizona. It's so much more relaxin' and homey here, surrounded by Todd, Willow, Piper, and Trig (with Gramps and the Ice Queen far away on the other side of the country), and I just love bein' able to go into the kitchen whenever I wanna heat up a Hot Pocket or Cup o' Noodles.

My prep team keeps coachin' me to be myself and just let that Sarah Palin charm flow naturally like salmon returnin' to their spawnin' grounds. So that's exactly what I'm gonna do. Everyone's helpin' me cram like crazy for the most important final exam of my life. Piper helps me run through my flash cards, Willow tests me on the names of world leaders, Todd showed me how to write crib notes on my arm, and I've been doin' mock debates with Trig (who makes the most adorable faces when I say the word "maverick").

I'm really excited about the debate, except I have absolutely nothing to wear. We really need to make a special trip into town so us girls can do a little shopping at Lord & Taylor!!!

ZINGERS FOR JOE BIDEN

* "Hey Joe, whaddya know? Nothing! Ha!"
* "Why so slow, Joe?"
* "Say it ain't so, Joe."
* "~~Don't be such a ho, Joe.~~"
* "You're gettin' Sloppy, Joe."
* "Tell us about the time Franklin D. Roosevelt got on television in 1929 to talk about the Depression. I just love that story."
* "Those hair plugs sure do make ya look cute."
* "Looks like someone's been inhalin' way too many Amtrak fumes."

OCTOBER 1, 2008

Dear Diary,

I hate Katie Couric. I hate Katie

Couric. I hate Katie Couric.

NEWSPAPERS AND MAGAZINES THAT I SHOULD SAY I READ

(to Impress People)

- GUNS & AMMO
- MOOSE HUNTER MONTHLY
- ALASKA AIRLINES MAGAZINE
- AERIAL WOLF HUNTER
- SNOWMOBILE DIGEST
- NATIONAL ENQUIRER
- FOREIGN AFFAIRS (I bet they print some scandalous tidbits, like who Vladimir Putin is rearin' his head with)
- TIME (but only that one issue with me on the cover)

OCTOBER 2, 2008

Dear Diary,

I really knocked Joe Biden's socks off in tonight's debate by turnin' on that Sarah Palin charm that got me voted Miss Congeniality in the Miss Alaska Pageant! (I really deserved to win the Miss Alaska tiara, not runner-up!!!) But I'll really show those judges when I get elected Vice President, and after tonight's debate, I'm definitely back in the saddle.

That Gwen Ifill asked a bunch of questions I just wasn't expectin' at all. But I don't think anyone noticed how I changed the subject so smoothly and talked about stuff I've been studyin' every day for the last week and how Gramps and I are gonna go to Washington not

embracin' status-quo politics-as-usual but to
do some reformin' and shake things up and take
on the good ol' boys! There was no way I was
gonna let all that studyin' go to waste.

   Funny, now that the debate is over, I can't
remember all that info I had crammed into
my little ol' head. It's like it went in my ears
and just spilled out at the debate, never to be
seen again. I just know I winked and smiled a
lot more than Joe Biden did, which people just
eat up, and that's what wins debates really,
like when John F. Kennedy looked so handsome
versus Richard Nixon, who looked like Oscar
the Grouch. I just know I looked really
adorable, and afterwards, Gwen Ifill said she
just loved my earrings, which was her way of
sayin' I was the winner! Oh yeah! Not too
shabby! You go, girl!

OCTOBER 4, 2008

Dear Diary,

   The campaign has really picked up speed!
I go from a hotel to an SUV to a campaign
rally (where I give my speech) to the No
Talk Express (where I watch TOP GUN) to a
campaign fundraiser (where I make the same
speech) to a campaign jet (where I watch TOP

GUN again and say a prayer to thank God that Gramps isn't the pilot) to another campaign rally (where I make the same speech yet again) to a different hotel. It's really an exhaustin' whirlwind tour, but the thousands of folks chantin' "Sarah, Sarah, Sarah!" and "Drill, baby, drill!" are really neat and make me feel so proud to be a hockey mom!!! It's just really hard bein' on the campaign trail and bein' Governor of Alaska at the same time.

I can't believe I've gotten so famous that Tina Fey keeps impersonatin' me on SATURDAY NIGHT LIVE. She's become soooooo popular for dressin' up like me and imitatin' the way I talk. I don't know why people laugh at her. Everything she said on last night's show in the fake debate made perfect sense to me. She really could be me! I really thought the guy who impersonated Joe Biden made him look like a total fool. I wonder if Tina Fey would be willin' to go to Alaska and pretend she's the Governor while I'm on the campaign trail. That way, I could actually be in two places at once, and Tina Fey would be too busy with the ~~Troopergate~~ Tasergate investigation to be on SATURDAY NIGHT LIVE every week and they'd only be able to make fun of Joe Biden!!!

THE VICE PRESIDENT SHOULD HAVE EXPANDED POWERS TO:

* Ban books from public libraries and schools
* Fire Alaska State Troopers
* Ignore subpoenas
* Make amendments to the Constitution at will
* Cancel SATURDAY NIGHT LIVE
* Label Tina Fey an enemy combatant and lock her up at Gitmo
* Wear a Wonder Woman costume to preside over Senate meetings

OCTOBER 5, 2008

Dear Diary,

It's not easy stayin' in touch with what's goin' on back home in Alaska while I'm crisscrossin' the country on the No Talk Express, but Talis Colberg, my Attorney General whiz kid back in Alaska, has really been doin' the Lord's work for me. Last week, he sued to get the Anchorage superior court to kill all those pesky subpoenas, but the judge (obviously some atheist left-wing liberal who sides with the terrorists) said no. Talis called to tell me the bad news. Now seven members of my staff who originally refused to honor their subpoenas have changed their minds and are gonna testify in the Tasergate investigation. Those dirty, no-good traitors! I told Todd that we should get Wooten to taser each and everyone of them until they agree not to testify, but Todd said that might backfire on us. Instead, he hopped on his snowmobile and went out to egg their houses. I love it!

OCTOBER 7, 2008

Dear Diary,

My speechwriter Scully showed me the story in today's NEW YORK TIMES that says Barack Obama served on the same education boards there in Chicago with Bill Ayers, who helped start up the Weathermen. I couldn't understand how reporting the weather could be a bad thing. When I was a sportscaster on KTUU-TV in Anchorage, I thought the weatherman was a really nice fella. But Scully explained that the Weathermen were an underground group that bombed buildings back there in the Sixties. Yikes!!! I guess they musta been really upset with the weather forecast.

Now I'm havin' a blast making speeches accusin' Barack Obama of bein' a shifty little devil who pals around with terrorists. It's really fun to take off the gloves and put on the heels! The stiletto heels! The really cool part is that now everyone thinks I read the NEW YORK TIMES every day! It's a double whammy!

Tonight Gramps and Obama have their second debate, but I'm so pooped from takin' off the gloves and puttin' on the heels, I'm gonna spend the night here in my hotel room takin' a warm bubble bath and doin' my nails. If I do watch any TV tonight, it's gonna be PROJECT RUNWAY.

OCTOBER 10, 2008

Dear Diary,

OMG!!! I can't believe the Alaska Legislative Council unanimously voted to release the Branchflower Report today! I thought Gramps and his lawyers would make sure the report wasn't released until way after the election. Oh well. The good news is that the report is 263 pages long. No one in her right mind is gonna read a 263-page report. I'm never gonna read it, that's for sure, even though it's all about my favorite person— me!!! And if I'm never gonna read it, that means no one else will either. Ha!

From what I hear, the report says that I abused the power of the Governor's office (Duh!) by pressurin' Monegan to fire Wooten

(Duh again!). Tell me something I don't already know! The report also says that one of the reasons I fired Monegan was most likely because he refused to fire Wooten (Duh for the third time!), but I had every right as Governor to fire Monegan for whatever reason I pleased (Duh! Duh! Duh! Duh!). So, as that great American, Joseph Goebbels would say, "I'm pleased to be cleared of any legal wrongdoing or any unethical activity."

And if anyone says the report found me guilty of abusin' power, I'm just gonna say the Alaskan Legislative Council are a bunch of partisan Barack Obama supporters who were out to get me! Who's gonna check up to see that the council is made up of ten elected Republicans and four elected Democrats? The same exact people who are gonna read that 263-page report. No one, that's who!!!

OCTOBER 15, 2008

Dear Diary,

Who the heck is Joe the Plumber? Todd and I are cooped up here in this hotel room in Manchester, New Hampshire, and I just wasn't in the mood to drill, baby, drill, so Todd turned on the TV to watch some ESPN. As he was flippin' through the channels, he landed on the final debate between Gramps and Obama, so we watched that for a while, and Gramps kept givin' shout-outs to Joe the Plumber—just like the way I do with Joe Six-Pack, except that Joe the Plumber is a real-live person somewhere in America.

Gramps called out Joe the Plumber so many times that I thought he forgot all about little ol' me and how much I've energized the ticket. I started to worry that maybe Gramps wants to dump me off the ticket and run with Joe the Plumber as his VP, that maybe Todd should give Wooten a call to see what he can do about this Joe the Plumber.

But Todd told me to relax, that I have nothing to worry about, that Gramps loves me to pieces—that the worst that could happen is that Gramps would appoint Joe the Plumber as Secretary of State or something. I think Secretary of the Interior would make more sense, so then Joe the Plumber could fix the drips in the White House. Of course, when we get elected there will only be one drip in the White House. Cindy McCain!!! Haha!

The crazy thing is: I think Joe the Plumber won the debate!

Dear Diary,

I didn't have to do a thing! I'm still the Republican candidate for Veep!!! The Gotcha Media took care of Joe the Plumber for me! Turns out he's not a licensed plumber, his name isn't Joe (it's Samuel J. Wurzelbacher!!!), and he owes back taxes!!! So, my job is safe, just like Todd said. But now I'm thinkin', with all the media attention Joe the Plumber is gettin', he'd be a perfect Vice Presidential candidate when I run for President!!! Palin/Plumber '12!!!

I saw the video clip of Joe the Plumber tellin' Barack Obama that he wants to buy the plumbing company he works for. When Joe asked if Obama would raise his taxes if he made over $250,000 a year, Obama said he thinks it's better to "spread the wealth around." That sounded pretty good to me, until some of the guys on my prep team told me that "spreadin' the wealth" sounds a lot like socialism. That scared me to pieces, because the only cure for socialism is penicillin, and now I'm petrified that if Obama gets elected President, he's gonna give everyone VD. That's just so wrong. Thank God that Joe the Plumber got Obama to spill his evil plan. Joe the Plumber is an American hero, just like my friends Joe Six-Pack and Joe Goebbels. I've gotta give shout-outs to more workin' American heroes! I'm not gonna blink!!! Wink, sure, but definitely not blink!

FRIENDS of JOE the PLUMBER

▶ Sid the Salesman   ▶ Frank the Fedex Guy
▶ Pete the Pool Cleaner   ▶ Chuck the Cashier
▶ George the Gardner   ▶ Larry the Cable Guy
▶ Ed the Electrician   ▶ Dora the Explorer

OCTOBER 17, 2008

Dear Diary,

I'm so glad that Todd's havin' a great time on the campaign trail. Today, he toured the Arctic Cat snowmobile factory there in Minnesota, so he was like a kid in a candy store.

I know he got a big kick a few days ago when Hank Williams, Jr. sang his song "Family Tradition" at our rally in Virginia Beach and changed the lyrics to "McCain-Palin Tradition" and sang about how I'm gonna take off my gloves and not blink and how I'm a good-lookin' dish, which really made Todd smile. Todd loves the original song, and he thought it was strange to hear such a patriotic version, since Hank's original lyrics talk about his love of drinkin' Jim Beam and smokin' that marijuana.

But anywho, tomorrow, while I'm rehearsin' to be a guest on SATURDAY NIGHT LIVE (I'm so famous!!!), Todd will be hostin' a tailgate party with the No Talk Express at the Penn State-Michigan homecomin' football game, complete with Moose Burgers—Todd's rocket fuel! He figured this way, if anything happens to Tina Fey while I'm on SATURDAY NIGHT LIVE, he has an air-tight alibi.

OCTOBER 18, 2008

Dear Diary,

When I arrived on the set of SATURDAY NIGHT LIVE, the first thing I did was ask Lorne Michaels if I could do a skit on the show where I'm waterboardin' Tina Fey. Lorne wanted some time to think about it, so in the meantime, he asked Alec Baldwin to entertain me for a while.

Alec took me to the green room and mixed up the tastiest drink! A Pink Russian! It's made from one part vodka and three parts Pepto-Bismol. It was yummy! The great thing is—if you drink too much, you don't get nauseous! He made me a few of them, and we were gettin' along just great.

I knew I'd fit right in there at SNL because I smoked some of that marijuana when it was legal back home in Alaska (unless you count federal laws, which Todd said didn't count if you're a member of the American Independence Party—as he passed me the bong). I didn't like how the pot made me feel (I thought everyone there in the room was out to get me, they were all starin' at me with jealousy in their eyes, and I just wanted to fire everyone, even though I was only in high school and no one worked for me yet), but I'm still very, very hip (especially with my spiffy new clothes) and I just knew Tina Fey and I would be BFFs.

Well, finally, Lorne Michaels found me there in the green room and explained that AFTRA rules prohibit anyone from waterboardin' Tina Fey on the show, but since I'm not a member of AFTRA, Tina Fey is totally allowed to waterboard me, if I'm willin' to do that. Alec Baldwin thought the idea was great and would really kill, which had me very worried until Lorne explained that "kill" means "get huge laughs."

Alec said Americans would just love to see Tina Fey waterboard me. They'd eat it up, he said. He rounded up some of the cast members, who all thought the idea was hysterical. Kenan volunteered to be the water boy, who keeps bringin' water to Tina, but keeps spillin' it everywhere. Andy immediately went to work writin' a parody of a Beach Boys song, called "Waterboardin' USA." Kristen wanted to play the fast-talkin' security guard who straps me in. Even Alec wanted to get in on the act, sayin' he'd play the good cop as Tina interrogated me as the bad cop. Everyone was so excited, and I was feelin' pretty good from all those Pink Russians—how could I say no?

Before I knew it, we were rehearsin' the sketch. I was lyin' on a plank of wood propped across two sawhorses. Kristen strapped me down and covered my head with a towel. The band started playin' "Waterboardin' USA," and Andy and some of the other guys, dressed like Uncle Sam in top hats and jackets sequined in red, white, and blue, were dancin' and singin' the song. Kenan carried the first bucket of water over to me, but he suddenly tripped, spillin' the entire bucket on the towel coverin' my face, and—oh my goodness!—I felt like I was drownin'! I couldn't breathe! I thought I was suffocatin' for sure!

Alec pulled the towel off my face, and I was coughin' and gaggin', and they all sat me up and I suddenly hurled pink Pepto-Bismol everywhere and on everyone!!! The guys from the McCain Team (Lorne called them the McTeam) immediately interrupted the rehearsal and said the waterboardin' was fine, but havin' me barf Pepto-Bismol all over the place on national TV would be really bad for the campaign, and so they killed the entire sketch. Just like that!!!

So then I told Lorne about the day a bunch of us in my office dressed up like Alaskan State Troopers and did a dance number to the ABBA song "Super Trouper," and I started singing my "Stupid Trooper" lyrics. Lorne said he really loved it, but for some reason he wanted to do something else instead.

I think even without the waterboardin' sketch, the show went really great. I never got a chance to speak with Tina, but I just know how grateful she is to me for launchin' her career and for inspirin' her to give herself such a terrific makeover by dressin' like me and doin' her hair like mine. She just adores me. She really does. I just know she's my number one fan!!!

Dear Diary,

What a crazy day! I gave a campaign speech to 10,000 folks in an airport hanger there in Roswell, New Mexico, which was kind of freaky. People say that UFOs crashed in Roswell in 1947, and I thought for sure that when the McTeam brought me to an airport hangar and told me that I'd be speakin' to the Republican base, the place would be filled with aliens. I was so relieved to find crowds of ordinary Americans, with just a small group of aliens sittin' behind me on the stage. The creepy thing is that one of them looked exactly like Cindy McCain!!! I was really glad to get the heck out of there!

While I'm out here campaignin' in Colorado and Nevada, Todd is back on the East Coast, where he was an honorary official for the NASCAR race at Martinsville Speedway there in Virginia. He's never been to a NASCAR race before because we don't have any racetracks back home in Alaska, but he fell in love with it, and said he wants to get behind the wheel of the No Talk Express and really open her up on the highway. I love that man to pieces. He's such a . . . . . MAN!

Dear Diary,

I respect Colin Powell, I really do. He's a great man, a great Republican, a great military leader, and a great big pain in the butt for sayin' I'm unqualified to be Vice President. What the heck does he know anyhow? He's the guy who got up there in front of the United Nations and swore that Saddam Hussein had weapons of mass destruction. He was dead wrong about that! What a goofball!!! I'm qualified, by golly. I was Mayor of Wasilla, I'm Governor of the biggest state in the United States, I've energized the Republican base, I've made chitchat with Henry Kissinger, I've watched TOP GUN a gazillion times, I've got killer dress suits from Sak's Fifth Avenue, and the First Dude of Alaska thinks I'm the cat's pajamas!!! So it's time for this hockey mom to slip into something more comfortable!

OCTOBER 22, 2008

Dear Diary,

I love my life!!! Everyday I give speeches before thousands and thousands of folks, and they just love me so much! This is so much better than winnin' the Miss Wasilla Beauty

Pageant, or the election for Mayor, or even the election for Governor!!! There are cameras and news teams and thousands of folks cheerin'!!! It's like Todd and I have been elected king and queen of the senior prom!!! I can't wait to be ~~President~~ Vice President!!! I'll wear a bright red sash that says "Ms. ~~President~~ Vice President" and a tiara with diamonds, and wherever I go, the Secret Service will roll out the red carpet, and folks will cheer like crazy because they love me to pieces because I'm such a maverick and I really shake things up!!!

OCTOBER 24, 2008

Dear Diary,

Just as I was about to be introduced to give my stump speech at a campaign rally there in Springfield, Missouri, Bristol called on my BlackBerry (that's when I discovered that Todd changed my ringtone from "Super Trouper" to "And the Cradle Will Rock" as a practical joke—not so funny in the middle of a campaign rally!!!). Bristol was all upset because Levi, the high school drop-out, enrolled in an apprenticeship program to be trained as an electrician. I guess bein' tasered really did shock some sense into the f***in' redneck.

"Listen, I'm about to make a speech, can I call ya right back after I call Barack Obama a socialist, John McCain a maverick, and Joe the Plumber a great American?"

When I got back aboard the No Talk Express, I locked myself in the bathroom and called Bristol for a girl-to-girl talk. There's nothing like tryin' to talk sense into a teenage girl whose hormones are ragin' like Hurricane Gustav because she's a teenage girl _and_ she's seven months pregnant. I was just thankin' the Lord that Bristol was back home in Alaska and not ridin' around with us on the No Talk Express with her hormones goin' gaga.

Bristol was cryin' like a wounded moose because Levi's father got him into the electrical apprenticeship program there in the Milne Point oil field on Alaska's North Slope. The job starts next week, which means Levi will be more than 800 miles away on the North Slope— not home in Wasilla, not on the hockey team at Wasilla High School, not there in Bristol's bedroom lightin' candles to worship Satan (thank goodness!). Poor sweet Bristol was just heartbroken. Well, that's what happens when you break your oath of abstinence. Hearts get broken. Dreams get broken. Campaign promises get broken. But the good news is that Levi is enrolled online to get his high school diploma. So I said, look honey, at least he'll be online so you two can be Instant Messagin' all the time. Ya gotta look at the bright side, bring positive change, be a maverick, take on the good ol' boys, and shake things up!

Dear Diary,

Oopsey daisy! A federal jury just convicted sweet old Senator Ted Stevens on seven felony charges for failin' to report gifts received from a big oil company. He could get up to 35 years in prison, which could really kill his chances of bein' reelected next week. Well, he's only 84-years old now. He can always run for the Senate again when he gets out of prison at age 129.

He really is a shady old coot, but he always helped me out. I love him like a perverted old uncle who gave me a shiny new Kennedy half-dollar and then wanted me to sit on his lap. He endorsed me for Governor, he helped us get earmarks for Wasilla, he appointed me to his 527 group, and we've held press conferences together. But Ted knows that I can't have folks thinkin' I pal around with criminals, so

I'm sure he won't mind that I badmouthed him today in a speech on the runway at the Richmond airport for takin' gifts from a big oil company that's part of the culture of corruption that I was elected to shake up. He knows it's nothing personal when I said I hope he does the right thing for Alaska. Of course, knowing Ted, he may think I'm tellin' him to accept more gifts from oil companies.

OCTOBER 28, 2008

Dear Diary,

Ted Stevens hasn't resigned yet, which is makin' him look like my own personal Bill Ayers and Reverend Jeremiah Wright rolled into one. So, before things spin out of control like a snowmobile hittin' a patch of ice, I released a statement callin' on dear sweet Ted to resign from the Senate. I felt just terrible for doin' it, kind of like Jesus turnin' Judas over to the Romans, but I had the McTeam write the statement so Ted could save face and "do the statesman-like thing" by "steppin' aside." It really doesn't matter if he resigns, since the election is next week anyway, and there's no way he's gonna win now — so I come out smellin' like a ~~rose~~ forget-me-not (the Alaska state flower)!

Dear Diary,

What a wild night! After an exhilaratin' campaign rally in Jefferson, Indiana, we piled back on the No Talk Express with our good friend Joe the Plumber, who we picked up early this morning at his house outside Toledo, Ohio. What a hottie!

Joe traveled with us to three campaign rallies in Ohio today, and he was hitchin' a ride with us to the next stop on the campaign trail. Joe got to talkin' with Todd, who claimed to be the real Joe Six-Pack, except we don't have any six-packs on the No Talk Express. So Todd told the driver to pull over so we could get some beer, and the next thing I knew, we were in the parkin' lot of a bar on the outskirts of Jefferson, Indiana, and Todd insisted that we all go inside for a little well-deserved rest and relaxation.

We piled off the RV (leavin' Willow on board to baby-sit Piper and Trig) and went inside the bar, which reminded me a whole lot of the Mug-Shot Saloon back home in Wasilla, just a regular down-home bar filled with real Americans who were overjoyed to see me. My campaign team brought in a whole bunch of

McCain-Palin balloons and campaign buttons to pass out to all the Joe Six-Packs in the bar. After posin' for pictures with the good folks, we found a booth there in the back.

We ordered a few pitchers and the next thing I knew, Joe the Plumber and Todd were arm wrestlin' to see which one of them was the bigger man. People there in the bar were cheerin' and placin' bets on who would win. They were chantin' "First Dude, First Dude, First Dude!" and "Joe the Plumber! Joe the Plumber! Joe the Plumber!" I was rootin' for Todd, of course. He looked so manly, but, I have to admit, so did Joe the Plumber, with his muscles bulgin' from his arm. (I sure would love to tell him to "Drill, baby, drill!" I'm sure he could get my pipes unclogged in no time.)

Todd was winnin', but suddenly Joe the Plumber gave a powerful yank, pinnin' Todd's hand to the table and winnin' the arm wrestlin' match. He threw his fists into the air trium- phantly and then grabbed me and gave me a deep kiss, which was—wow!—something else. Todd was ready to punch Joe the Plumber in the mouth, but he suddenly noticed a guy usin' a cell phone to take video of Joe the Plumber kissin' me, and realizin' that the guy would probably post that video on YouTube the moment he got home or sell it to ENTERTAINMENT TONIGHT or something, Todd wrestled the guy to the ground, grabbed the cell phone, ran to the bathroom, and flushed it down the toilet. When he came back, he had that crazy fire in his eyes, and I thought he was gonna punch Joe the Plumber in the nose, but what I was seein' in his eyes was sheer panic.

The cell phone had clogged the toilet and water was now overflowin' there in the bathroom. Joe the Plumber pulled out his pipe wrench from his back pocket and volunteered to fix it, and off he darted to the restroom, which was very nice of him—although Todd said it was really his fault in the first place.

Suddenly folks in the bar were cheerin' "Sarah! Sarah! Sarah!" and I suddenly noticed a mechanical bull there in the corner of the bar and the crowd split like the Red Sea for me to pass through. The next thing I knew, the crowd hoisted me up on the saddle. Todd was takin' bets for how long I'd last. The machine switched on, and I found myself ridin' that crazy, buckin' bronco. The machine jolted and turned and tossed, and I threw my hands up in the air and yelled out "Yeee-haw!!!" Todd put some coins in the jukebox and the Van Halen song "And the Cradle Will Rock" filled the bar. Around and around I went, and the crowd was goin' wild, cheerin' "Thrill, baby, thrill!"

The bathroom door burst open, and it seemed like someone had opened a fire hydrant because water was blastin' out like a geyser. Joe the Plumber came stumblin' out, soaked from head to toe. He had loosened the wrong pipe or valve or something. Some of the regulars grabbed Joe and hauled him back into the bathroom, shoutin', "Joe, you better fix that plumbin'!" Joe hollered back, "But I'm not really a plumber and my name's really not Joe."

A loud bell rang and the mechanical bull stopped buckin', and cheers rose from the crowd! I had won, and Todd was collectin' wads of cash from folks! The campaign team quickly escorted us back outside and onto the No Talk Express, and as we pulled out of the parkin' lot, I could see police cars with their red lights flashin' pullin' into the parkin' lot. "Step on it!" yelled Todd, and our driver floored it and we pealed out of there. That's the last I saw of Joe the Plumber.

Willow, Piper, and Trig were fast asleep there in the back of the RV. They looked adorable.

Todd held up the wad of cash he had won from my ride on the mechanical bull.

"Oh yeah!" I exclaimed. "Neiman Marcus here we come!"

Dear Diary,

Ooops. Gramps called out for Joe the Plumber at a campaign rally this morning at Defiance Junior High School in Ohio, but Joe wasn't there. "Joe's with us today!" Gramps announced. "Joe, where are you? Where is Joe? Is Joe here with us today?" When I saw that on TV, I almost choked on my caribou sausage. I realized that we left No-Show Joe back at the bar in Indiana! How embarrassin'!!!

Fortunately, Joe caught up with Gramps this afternoon to be his mascot at the gazebo there in the town square of Sandusky, Ohio. I guess Joe got the cops to drive him over there. I sure do hope he fixed the pipes in that restroom!

Dear Diary,

We raced around Pennsylvania (Todd's been callin' it Transylvania in honor of Halloween), goin' from one campaign rally to the next—all day long. I've been tryin' to scare the bejesus out of folks, tellin' them the truth about the monster that is Barack Obama. He's the Muslim anti-Christ, the beast who's pallin' around with terrorists and who's gonna turn America into a socialist hell, where left-wing liberal zombies take away your guns and feed on the hard work of real no-nonsense Americans like Joe the Plumber. People just ate it up, especially with Piper standin' by my side dressed as an adorable little snow princess. She's such a honey.

Speakin' of honeys, the highlight of the day was meeting Mike Ditka, who coached the Chicago Bears to victory in the 1985 Super Bowl. His Super Bowl ring is just gorgeous. He was born there in Transylvania (now Todd's got me sayin' that) and to introduce me at the rally, he gave a great locker-room pep talk, tellin' the crowd to go out there and win one for the Gipper. He didn't actually say that, but that's what he meant, I'm sure.

The rally was at a hangar at the Arnold Palmer Regional Airport there in Labrobe, Pennsylvania, which is Arnold Palmer's hometown, and I took all that as a sign from God because the first house that Todd and I bought back home in Wasilla was on Arnold Palmer Drive (for real!), we love to drink Arnold Palmers, Trig was born in Palmer, Alaska, and if Track had been born on a golf course, we mighta named him Palmer (although Todd preferred the name Putts).

Another sign from God was that Tom Ridge, who was former Governor of Transylvania (there I go again) and the first Secretary of Homeland Security, kicked off the rally. It was so cool to be on stage with the guy who came up with that awesome Homeland Security threat level chart — with red alert, orange alert, yellow alert, and whatever the other colors are. With Barack Obama leadin' in the polls and pallin' around with terrorists, I told Tom Ridge that the country should really be on red alert. But Tom said he's no longer head of Homeland Security. Oh my gosh, who is?

NOVEMBER 1, 2008

Dear Diary,

I thought the skit Gramps did on SATURDAY NIGHT LIVE tonight alongside Tina Fey was just precious. It was great that Tina was willin' to substitute for me since I was busy on the campaign trail speakin' at rallies in Florida, North Carolina, and Virginia. I loved how Gramps and Tina pretended to be sellin' campaign products on QVC because we can't afford to run a half-hour campaign commercial on television like that socialist Barack Obama did this week. Tina really did a terrific job bein' me, especially when she went off to the side and held up a T-shirt sayin' "Palin 2012." That's exactly what I woulda done!

I almost fell out of my chair laughin' when Tina held up that Sarah Palin Ayers Freshener with a picture of Bill Ayers on it, for when things don't quite smell right. I think we really oughta look into marketin' those—to raise money for 2012!!!

NOVEMBER 3, 2008

Dear Diary,

I'm exhausted! We did six campaign rallies today, travelin' to five states in one day! When this election's over, all I wanna do is get out into nature, where it's nice and quiet, and shoot me some elk.

I did get reenergized this afternoon when the Alaska State Personnel Board released its own Tasergate report. The report blasts the Branchflower report and says there's no way I broke any laws by firin' Monegan or abused my power as Governor just because I let Todd and my aides hassle Monegan. I mean, really, the guy just shoulda fired Wooten, for cryin'-out loud. I'm so happy that my name has been cleared, and no one ever has to know that as Governor, I coulda fired the three members of the Alaska State Personnel Board if I wasn't pleased with their report. Fortunately, I don't have to fire anyone because their report totally rocks!!! And just in time for the big election tomorrow!!! Wow, talk about God's will!!!

I just know in my heart that God wants me to be President of the United States, but I just have to trust in the Lord and have faith that I'll be elected Vice President tomorrow (and become President when Gramps dies from pneumonia a month after I convince him to walk in the Inauguration Parade without a coat, or when he croaks in a compromisin' position on his desk there in the Oval Office). If we lose tomorrow (Heaven forbid!), then I'll know God plans for me to be elected President four years from now in 2012. Either way, God blesses America with me, his humble hockey mom, as President!

Dear Diary,

We flew into Alaska on the campaign jet early this morning so Todd and I could cast our votes at Wasilla City Hall, and as we drove along the highway, people lined the road there in the freezing cold, chantin' my name and wavin' signs. It was so excitin', and I just pray that when I wake up tomorrow morning, I'll be the new Vice President . . . even though, oh dear Diary, forgive me, but when I got in the voting booth and closed the curtain, as excited as I was to see my name — Governor Sarah Palin!!! — on the ballot for Vice President of the United States, I just felt horrible for all the terrible things I said about Barack Obama, bless his heart, callin' him a socialist and sayin' he palled around with terrorists, when he really does inspire so much hope, and he's got so much more youth and charisma than Gramps, and his wife Michelle is so much sweeter than the Ice Queen, and I figured, well, it is a secret ballot, so no one will ever know who I voted for, and one little ol' vote in Alaska ain't gonna get Barack Obama elected President — although I did get a little worried when Todd and Bristol told me they had done the same thing!!!

Todd and I took all the kids on the campaign jet to Phoenix, Arizona, where we were gonna watch the election results with Gramps and the Ice Queen and then have a big celebration at the Biltmore Hotel. But the polls were lookin' really bad, and I knew we didn't stand a snowball's chance in hell of winnin' the election. So when Gramps and the Ice Queen met us at the Phoenix Airport, I told Gramps that I wanted to give a speech tonight, no matter whether we win or lose, to really put myself on the map. This was my golden moment, to really shine as next in line for the Republican nomination for President in 2012.

But Gramps got all crotchety and said no way, this was his golden moment, and it just wasn't appropriate for me to make a speech. But I was totally psyched to give my speech, and when I'm totally psyched to give a speech that's gonna put me on the map and launch me into the big time, nothing stands in my way— not even if I'm pregnant and my water has broken and I'm feelin' contractions!!! I felt just like Maverick in TOP GUN, which gave me a great idea.

"Why don't we settle this with a good ol' fashioned dog fight?" I asked.

"We don't have any dogs," said Gramps. "Although you really are a pit bull, my friend."

"No, no, a dogfight in airplanes," I explained. "Just like in TOP GUN."

"TOP GUN?" asked Gramps, his eyes lightin' up and twinklin'.

"You're a pilot. Todd's a pilot. We've got two jet planes. Let's take this to the skies. If Todd wins, I make my speech."

"And if I win?" asked Gramps.

I gave him my famous wink.

The next thing I knew, Todd and I and the kids were takin' off again in our campaign jet with Todd at the wheel. We were blastin' that song "Highway to the Danger Zone" over the sound system, and we were doin' all sorts of barrel rolls and loop-de-loops and nosedives. The kids loved it! It was just like a rollercoaster ride for them.

I had a shotgun, and I opened the window and started shootin' at Gramps and the Ice Queen as they flew by doin' a barrel roll of their own. Blam! Blam! It was just like aerial huntin' for wolves, except Gramps was the wolf. Blam! Blam! Blam!

Suddenly Todd yelled out that I had accidentally shot one of our engines!!! The doggone thing was on fire. Flames were shootin' out from the engine and the sky was filled with black smoke.

I've been huntin' all my life, and I definitely know how to use a gun, so I don't see how I could have possibly shot the engine of our plane. It's like I was bein' accused of bringin' down our plane, just like the left-wing liberal Gotcha Media accused me of bringin' down the McCain campaign. I knew that couldn't possibly be true, because folks love me, they really do, they line up hours ahead of time for my rallies and they cheer "Sarah, Sarah, Sarah!" Then I remembered the harsh stare from the Ice Queen's eyes, and it suddenly hit me that she somehow used her alien powers and shot some sort of laser beam from her steely cold eyes to set our engine on fire. I'm sure of it. It's the only logical explanation.

Our plane started spinnin' out of control. "Eject! Eject!" shouted Todd. "I'm sorry, honey, but it looks like you won't be makin' any speeches tonight."

Todd and me and the kids parachuted from the plane, with me holdin' baby Trig in my arms. As we floated down, I watched our campaign jet crash out there in the Arizona desert, and I got a little teary eyed thinkin' of all the time we had spent on that plane, flyin' around the country. I could see the glimmerin' lights of Phoenix stretched below me. It looked so beautiful, like a thousand points of light or a shinin' city on a hill.

Todd and I landed on the big lawn there in front of the Biltmore Hotel, where a huge crowd of fans was waitin' for us to arrive. They went wild, cheerin' like crazy, blown away by our entrance. "Sarah, Sarah, Sarah!" they chanted, followed by a chorus of "First Dude! First Dude! First Dude!" and "Trig! Trig! Trig!" I think parachutin' into the hotel was better than any speech I could have given!!!

A while later, the Straight Talk Express pulled up and Gramps gave his concession speech. It brought me to tears thinkin' that I was this close to bein' a boink away from the Presidency, and it tore me up inside knowin' that Gramps wouldn't let me give a rousin' speech to get folks excited about 2012! The Republican Party really shot itself in the foot by not lettin' me rally the troops—because this little ol' hockey mom is ready to take back the White House ASAP! You betcha!

MY CONCESSION SPEECH

My fellow real Americans,

Tonight the American people have made a terrible mistake by electin' a socialist—who pals around with terrorists and wants to take away your guns and force your daughters to have abortions—to the highest office in the land. But dontcha worry! Four years from now, I'm gonna shake things up so we can take back the White House! Because I've put my life in God's hands and He's given me the lipstick to do it! And the wardrobe! This hockey mom doesn't take the referee's word for it. She goes out on the ice and fights for what's right!!!

John McCain, bless his heart, is a true American hero, a man who faced great adversity at Annapolis and graduated at the bottom of his class, who courageously dumped his first wife to marry an heiress, who knows how to be a maverick among mavericks. Let us thank the Almighty Creator for this man, who put his country first and plucked me out of the Alaskan tundra to save our party, to save our country, and to save the free world—from left-wing liberals who want to spread the wealth and have us believe that good, patriotic Americans like Joe the Plumber evolved from monkeys. To that, I say no. No, no, no, no, no. Why do I say no? Because this is America, and, by golly, we're better than that.

I won't stop fightin' until we've broken though that glass ceiling and I'm elected President of the United States. Because breakin' through that glass ceiling means job creation—hirin' thousands of people to clean up all those pieces of glass. Breakin' through the glass ceiling means better health care—gettin' doctors to help all the people who cut themselves on the shards of glass. Breakin' through the glass ceiling means energy independence—takin' on the good ol' boys in the oil companies by lettin' that big ol' sun shine through the gapin' hole there in the roof.

So my fellow Americans, ask not why we lost the election, but ask what you can do to elect Sarah Palin President in 2012! Thank you! And God bless ~~Alaska~~ America!

NOVEMBER 7, 2008

Dear Diary,

Well, here I am, back home in Wasilla. Dullsville, U.S.A. Everything seems so small and slow and insignificant. I got all dolled up this morning and drove into the Governor's office in

Anchorage for the first time in two months, and I was all excited to be greeted by the press and get a hero's welcome. I was expectin' throngs of folks waitin' on line for hours to see me, chantin' "Sarah, Sarah, Sarah," and wavin' posters, givin' me that amazin' rush of adrenaline, but no one was there but five or six cameramen, some local TV correspondents, and a reporter from the ALASKA DAILY NEWS. There were no balloons, no confetti, no marchin' bands. I felt like I went from Republican rock star to Republican has-been in the wink of an eye.

When I walked into my office, I couldn't believe that the good folks who had been holdin' down the fort and keepin' their noses to the grindstone looked like they had gotten their clothes at Goodwill. I guess they've never seen the inside of Neiman Marcus, Sak's Fifth Avenue, Bloomingdale's, or Lord & Taylor.

It felt really good to be back in the saddle and I was lookin' forward to havin' lots to do there in the Governor's office and bein' able to concentrate on bein' a full-time Governor, but there really wasn't that much to do now that the whole Tasergate investigation has ended, and the McTeam isn't here to pester me all the time, and I don't have to go to any campaign

CAMPAIGN SLOGANS FOR 2012!

* Get Wailin' with Palin
* Go Whalin' with Palin
* Go Sailin' with Palin
* Let Palin Do the Jailin'
* Failin'? Vote Palin.
* The Barracuda is Back!
* Baked Alaska '12
* Palin Power
* Drill, Sarah, Drill!
* Join the Palin Pipeline
* Todd for First Dude '12
* Sarah Palin. The Bridge to the White House.

rallies, or turn away TV interviews, or meet with any more foreign leaders. I guess I could always go to Lamaze classes with Bristol. She does need a coach now that Levi's up on the North Slope.

The polls are showin' that I'm the number one choice for the 2012 Republican Presidential nomination, so if Bristol doesn't want me as her Lamaze coach, I guess I could always open up my Presidential campaign headquarters. I'm sure I'd have a blast decoratin' it!

PRODUCTS I COULD ENDORSE IN TV COMMERCIALS

- BLACK & DECKER DRILLS ("Drill, baby, drill!")
- COVERGIRL LIPSTICK ("What's the difference between a hockey mom and a pit bull?")
- BUSHNELL BINOCULARS (for seein' Russia)
- LENSCRAFTERS (my stylish specs, of course)
- CLAIROL NICE 'N EASY HIGHLIGHTING
- HAMBURGER HELPER (for Moose Burgers — pshaw!)

NOVEMBER 11, 2008

Dear Diary,

It's been really nice to be back in the white-hot spotlight again! On Sunday, Greta Van Susteren came over to the house to interview me for FOX NEWS, which was really sweet of her. I love bein' free to do as many media interviews as I please without bein' held back on a leash. Yesterday, I did an interview with Matt Lauer for the TODAY SHOW. He really is a cutie. I'd love to match him up with my sister Molly. She could really use a man around the house. Too bad he's married. Oh well, that's the way it goes.

Hangin' out with Matt and all the NBC cameramen reminded me how much fun I had on SATURDAY NIGHT LIVE, so today I called Lorne Michaels to ask if Tina Fey would like to trade places with me for a while, like in THE PRINCE AND THE PAUPER (the Disney movie with Mickey Mouse, not the book by Mark Twain—which I'm sure should be banned). If Tina and I switched places, no one would be able to tell the difference! I'd get the heck out of this one-horse town, Tina would have a great time bein' Governor, and I'd have lots of fun bein' back with the gang on SNL.

Lorne's secretary said that Lorne was in a meeting for the foreseeable future, and besides, she said, Tina isn't a regular on SNL anymore. She stars on her own show 30 ROCK, which I betcha I could do, because after all, I've been on SNL too, ya know, and I have a degree in communications/journalism and I starred as a television sportscaster on KTUU-TV here in Anchorage.

The secretary also said that Tina was really busy because she just got a book deal for $6 million, and then I thought wow, what a great idea, I should get a book deal, too. If a publisher was willin' to pay $6 million for Tina's book, they'd pay at least $6 gazillion for mine, since I'm the real deal, not some cheap imitation. After all, Tina's just cashin' in on my popularity. I'm the star!!! And I've been keepin' this diary, so all I gotta do is have Piper type this up, leave out some of the personal stuff, and add some of my serious political thoughts to give the Republican Party direction and get people revved up to elect me President in 2012. Hmm, serious political thoughts. Where am I gonna get those? Hmmmm. Let's see...

When I was the Mayor of Wasilla, I kept a big glass jar on my desk filled with pieces of paper with the name of every citizen of Wasilla. Once a week, I'd close my eyes, stick my hand in the jar, and pull out a piece of paper, and call that person, and ask "How am I doin' as Mayor?" When I'm elected President, I'm gonna keep a jar on my desk with the names of every citizen of the United States, and once a week, I'm gonna call one lucky American.

Other ideas:

TAXES: Instead of assessin' taxes accordin' to how much a person earns, we should assess taxes accordin' to how much a person weighs. Thin people should pay less in taxes than fat people who take up more room. This plan will also encourage millions of overweight Americans to lose weight (and lower the amount of body

POSSIBLE TITLES for my BOOK

- READ MY LIPSTICK
- REVENGE OF CARIBOU BARBIE
- I AM SARAH, HEAR ME ROAR
- THE ONE BOOK THAT SHOULD NEVER BE BANNED
- A FAREWELL TO WOLVES
- THE PALIN MANIFESTO
- FEAR AND LOATHING IN WASILLA
- SARAH PALIN SUPERSTAR
- THE SARAH PALIN POP-UP BOOK
- THE GOVERNOR'S NEW CLOTHES
- SNOW BLIND AMBITION
- I'LL GET BACK TO YOU ON THAT
- BRISTOL'S MOM: THE BARRACUDA SPEAKS
- CONFESSIONS OF A HOCKEY MOM
- MY FACE IS UP HERE (IN ALASKA!)

heat they generate, which will help reduce global warming).

GLOBAL WARMING: If every American turned on their air-conditioner full blast and opened all the doors and windows, we'd end global warming in a week—or two weeks tops. If you don't have an air-conditioner, you can open your refrigerator and freezer doors. We can start an "Open Your Hearts, Open Your Windows Foundation" to buy air-conditioners for folks that don't have one, as long as they promise to open their windows and doors. We're Americans. We can get this global warming under control!!!

THE HOMELESS: The homeless shouldn't be called homeless in the first place. America is their home. They should be called Americans. This will drastically reduce the number of homeless people overnight.

NOVEMBER 13, 2008

Dear Diary,

It's great to be out of Alaska and back here in the lower 48 in the limelight again, gettin' the attention I deserve! I was really a big hit here today with my fellow Republican Governors (all 21 of us!!!) as the featured speaker at the Republican Governors Conference in Miami. I totally stole the show with my speech about the future of the Republican Party, which finally gave me a chance to use some of my concession speech and let my fellow Governors know that the future of the Republican Party is right here with little ol' me.

If God opens that door for me in 2012 (and I pray to sweet Jesus that He will), I'm ready to plow right through to the White House. I just love bein' here in Miami because it's great to be out in front of the lights again and, unlike Alaska, it stays light outside past 2 o'clock in the afternoon!!!

NOVEMBER 14, 2008

Dear Diary,

Ughh!!! I hate bein' back in the black-hole darkness of Alaska. Everything seems so trivial here. A few weeks from now is the 50th anniversary of Alaskan statehood, so tonight was a formal dinner at the only snazzy hotel in Anchorage in honor of all the past Governors of Alaska. Every livin' Governor showed up (although some of them seemed kinda dead to me). We watched a ten-minute movie about the history of Alaska that was ten-minutes too long, and each one of us received a special commemorative gift in honor of Alaska's 50th Anniversary (I don't know what's so special about a plastic snow globe of the state capitol building, so I gave it to Willow who thinks it's really cool). We were promised headliner entertainment, which turned out to be a bunch of Eskimos doin' animal calls. Todd thought it was great. He turned to me and whispered,

"After a few beers, there's nothing I love more than hearin' wild moans and groans." That's my First Dude!

Dear Diary,

Boy, it's really difficult stayin' on the national scene when I'm weighted down by all the busywork of bein' Governor. It's like wearin' a ball and chain all day long. It really is. Today I had to give a speech to kickoff the Alaska Resource Development Council Convention, as if I really wanted to be in the same convention hall with a bunch of egghead Alaska energy producers and developers, bless their hearts. I really miss havin' 20, 30, 40, 50, 60,000 people cheerin' and wavin' signs and chantin' "Drill, baby, drill!"

I forced myself to sit through a really dull panel discussion about oil on the North Slope given by some wet blankets from BP and ConocoPhillips, and then I snuck the heck out of there. No way was I gonna waste the next two days sittin' through a whole bunch of borin' lectures about polar bears and pipelines. I've got Todd here at home to tell me what's up with all that stuff.

Dear Diary,

I'm sure glad I skipped out on the second day of that borin' Resource Development Council Convention. I didn't really need to hear the "Federal Update on Alaska Gas Pipeline Projects" or any more presentations from TransCanada or the Denali gas line. That stuff just puts me to sleep. Zzzzzzzzzzz. It's more important that I get myself on television for the world to see that I'm the obvious choice for President in 2012.

Thanksgiving is next week, so I went to the Triple-D Farm and Hatchery here in Wasilla to pardon a turkey—just like the President does—so people will see that I'm qualified to be President (not a turkey, Todd!). That's what people love to see! Sure enough, that got me on the 6 o'clock news. But after I pardoned the turkey, oh my gosh, I gave a television interview there at the farm with no idea that a few feet behind me one of the workers was slaughterin' a turkey. I did get a lot more national attention than I ever expected (I'm _soooo_ famous on YouTube!), which was cool, although I probably lost the vegetarian vote. It wasn't my fault though. It's that doggone Gotcha Media.

Next time, instead of me goin' to the turkey, the turkey comes to the Governor's office. I just didn't want people sayin' there's already a turkey in the Governor's office. Sometimes no matter whatcha do, you just can't win.

DECEMBER 5, 2008

Dear Diary,

Sorry it's been so long since I've written but things are really slow as molasses as we head into the dark abyss of winter. I went up to Fairbanks today for a ceremony to sign the papers to let TransCanada build that 1,700-mile pipeline from Alaska's North Slope to Alberta, Canada. So now the race is on to see if they can build their pipeline before those muckety-mucks at BP and ConocoPhillps build theirs. It's kinda exciting. I pray that TransCanada wins so we can show those big oil companies and the Gotcha Media who's really boss. Me!!!!

DECEMBER 12, 2008

Dear Diary,

Bristol came to me this afternoon, cryin' like a baby. At first I thought maybe she had gone into labor, but when I asked her what was wrong, all she could say was Levi, Levi, Levi.

The way she was cryin' I thought maybe he had electrocuted himself while workin' as an apprentice up there on the North Slope. Turns out Bristol was chattin' online with Levi, when all of a sudden, he typed that he doesn't wanna get married, that he wants to break off the engagement, although I'm not sure how you break off an engagement if you've got your fiancé's name tattooed to your ring finger. I guess Levi could always go back to the tattoo parlor and have the word "Myers" tattooed under the word Bristol, kinda like the way people get tattoos of the Harley-Davidson logo.

I can't believe Levi could be so two-faced. How on earth did he ever learn to be like that? Probably from that book on Satanism. Well, if Levi doesn't want to be First Slacker, Bristol will just have to find another slacker. I'm confident she can do that. No problem.

But Todd said not to worry, he'll come up with something to get Levi and Bristol back together. I just don't see Mike Wooten drivin' 800 miles up to the North Slope to taser the f***in' redneck. Todd is already facin' contempt charges before the Alaska Senate, so he figures he has nothing to lose. Well, if Levi doesn't want to make a honest woman out of

Bristol, then I guess Todd's right. We're just gonna have to apply some of that famous Palin pressure. I can't wait to see what Todd comes up with. We really are soul mates!

DECEMBER 18, 2008

Dear Diary,

I was there in my office in Anchorage, doin' my gubernatorial duties (I love that word, it reminds me of Goober on THE ANDY GRIFFITH SHOW), when Todd called up and said, "Quick! Turn on the TV news!" There on the TV, clear as day, I watched as Alaska State Troopers arrested Levi's mother, Sherry Johnston, right in front of her house, on six felony counts for dealin' Oxycontin.

"Wow," I said, "The Lord sure works in mysterious ways."

"Actually, Mike Wooten works in mysterious ways," said Todd. He told me how he persuaded the Stupid Trooper to turn up the heat on Levi's family. "All it took was a case of beer and his workers comp file."

We're back in the saddle, baby! When Levi sees his mother behind bars, he'll definitely have second thoughts about messin' with Sarah Barracuda. Oh yeah!

Dear Diary,

Yowza! Walt Monegan announced that he's runnin' for Mayor of Anchorage. That could mean he's thinkin' about runnin' for Governor down the road, like when I come up for re-election at the end of 2010. I just don't understand why that darn Monegan refuses to ride off quietly into the sunset. None of that Tasergate stuff woulda ever happened if that blasted Monegan hadn't been such a gosh-darn blabbermouth!!!

I don't hold any grudges against him, but instead of that turkey bein' slaughtered, it shoulda been Monegan, bless his heart! That woulda been a hoot! I do wish Monegan would take a hint already and make like the Arctic ice shelf and disappear.

DECEMBER 25, 2008

Dear Diary,

All I really wanted for Christmas was to be elected Vice President, so when Santa Claus reared his head and flew into Alaskan airspace last night, I was really tempted to pull out my shotgun and hunt me some reindeer. I figured that might be a bad way to show off my foreign policy know-how, so, instead, as Alaska's big cheese, I just kept a close eye on the situation because the last thing I needed on my hands was an invasion of elves from the North Pole.

I had a wonderful Christmas day, celebrating the birthday of the sweet baby Lord Jesus, surrounded by my beautiful family and our Christmas tree all decorated with leftover campaign buttons and a thousand points of light. Who could ask for more? Bristol dressed up like Santa Claus (at nine months, she's definitely got the big belly for it!) and handed out the presents. For his first Christmas, Trig got baby's first huntin' outfit and shotgun. Willow and Piper dressed him up and he looked absolutely adorable. Of course, it's tough celebratin' Christmas with Track bein' off in Iraq, but it's nice to know that he spent Christmas at the palace with my old friend Jalal Talabani, who cooked up Moose Burgers, just like he promised. Now that's Christmas spirit!

I also got a real surprise gift from the Republican National Committee. They sent over a Salvation Army truck, which was really sweet of them, to gather up my wardrobe. It's nice to know that the less fortunate will soon be as stylish as I am.

Best of all, Todd and I had a terrific surprise gift for Bristol. Levi ain't gonna have a job 800 miles away on the North Slope for very much longer!!! Turns out that federal regulations require anyone in an apprentice program to have a high school diploma—something the kid definitely doesn't have! When that little piece of information hits the news in a few days, Levi will have to come crawlin' back to Wasilla! Merry Christmas, Bristol!!!

DECEMBER 26, 2008

Dear Diary,

Goodness gracious, today was a miraculous day!!! Around noon, Bristol got all upset when she went down in the basement to find that all the bottles of beer that she and Levi had brewed up were missin'! Todd explained that he had given the beer to Wooten, which really confused Bristol.

"Well, I had to give him something to get him to bust Levi's mom," said Todd.

"I can't believe you did that!" yelled Bristol. "Now Levi will never want to speak with me again. You're ruinin' my life!"

Before Todd could explain, Bristol grabbed the car keys and ran out of the house. I heard the car peal out of the driveway.

"She'll be back," I said. "She just needs to blow off some steam."

A little while later, the doorbell rang. It was the Stupid Trooper. He held a big cardboard box filled with used hockey pucks.

"What's this all about?" I asked.

Todd grabbed two hockey sticks from the garage. He and Wooten were plannin' to go to downtown Anchorage to hit hockey pucks through the front window of Monegan's campaign headquarters. That sounded like a lot of fun to me, so I bundled up baby Trig in his new huntin' outfit, put him in his baby carrier, and we all snowmobiled together into downtown Anchorage.

It was dark by the time we got downtown, and when we pulled up across the street from the building, the lights were on in the campaign headquarters and we could see people inside. Todd and Wooten unloaded the box and lined up a row of hockey pucks on the snow-covered sidewalk. Todd grabbed a hockey stick and took the first whack, sendin' a puck flyin' into the plate glass window. It bounced off the glass with a loud bang. Everyone inside looked out the window, and suddenly I noticed Bristol inside.

She was wearin' a big "Monegan for Mayor" button and stuffin' envelopes for Monegan's campaign!!! I couldn't believe it! My mouth dropped open. My own flesh and blood had turned on me! For the first time in my life, I was speechless.

Suddenly Todd smacked another puck. It smashed through the glass window and there was a loud crash, and I saw the puck hit Bristol in the head. She fell to the floor. Todd and Wooten jumped on their snowmobiles to get the heck out of there, but I yelled, "That's Bristol!" and I ran across the street to the campaign headquarters, with baby Trig strapped to me, to see if my baby girl was okay. She was lyin' on the floor in a puddle of water, screamin' at the top of her lungs!!! The hockey puck had induced labor!!!

Todd carried Bristol outside and threw her on the back of his snowmobile. Baby Trig and I hopped on the back of Wooten's snowmobile, with me carryin' the hockey sticks, and we all raced the 45 miles to the Mat-Su Regional Medical Center in Palmer—with a side bet of a case of beer for whoever got there first. Wooten and I were in the lead, until I accidentally hit him in the head with one of the hockey sticks—which made baby Trig laugh hysterically. It was so cute! Todd and Bristol won the race, so Wooten is gonna give back the case of beer! So everything worked out great!

Dear Diary,

This morning at 5:30 a.m., Bristol gave birth to my first grandchild, Tripp Easton Mitchell Johnston—a beautiful baby boy, weighin' 7 pounds, 4 ounces. She named the baby Tripp in honor of the wild trip we made to the hospital. We Palin gals sure know how to have babies!!! She got the name Easton from the company that makes hockey gear, and Mitchell is the name of a company that makes fishin' rods and reels. Todd and I told her to give the kid the last name Johnston to ~~pressure~~ encourage the f***in' redneck to tie the knot (and make it easier for a judge to order him to pay child support)!

I can't believe I'm a grandmother and baby Trig is an uncle! Now all we gotta do is keep baby Tripp far away from his Oxycontin-dealin', beer-swillin', white-trash granny. Twenty years in the slammer should do the trick. I'll give Talis Colberg a call in the morning.

President Palin!

President Sarah Palin

PRESIDENT & MR. SARAH PALIN

President Ms. Sarah Palin

HER MAJESTY PRESIDENT
SARAH PALIN

MADAM PRESIDENT

HER ROYAL HIGHNESS PRESIDENT PALIN

MRS. PRESIDENT TODD PALIN

PRESIDENT MRS. TODD PALIN

PRESIDENT MOM

President Sarah Palin and First Dude Todd
President Sarah Palin President
President Sarah Palin!!! Yeah!

President Baracuda

www.ingramcontent.com/pod-product-compliance
Lightning Source LLC
Chambersburg PA
CBHW031513040426
42445CB00009B/201